COMING OF AGE IN TIMES OF UNCERTAINTY

COMING OF AGE IN TIMES OF UNCERTAINTY

Harry Blatterer

Berghahn Books
New York • Oxford

First published in 2007 by

Berghahn Books

www.berghahnbooks.com

© 2007 Harry Blatterer

Library of Congress Cataloging-in-Publication Data

Blatterer, Harry.
   Coming of age in times of uncertainty/ Harry Blatterer.
      p. cm.
   Includes bibliographical references and index.
   ISBN 1-84545-285-2 (hardback : alk. paper)
   1. Adulthood.   2. Social role.   3. Life cycle, Human.   I. Title.
HQ799.95.B56 2007
305.2409172'2—dc22   2006036156

British Library Cataloguing in Publication Data
A catalogue record for this book is available from the British Library

Printed in the United States on acid-free paper

ISBN: 978-1-84545-285-8   hardback

For Maria and Mira

Contents

	Preface	IX
	Acknowledgements	XIII
	Introduction	I
1	Representations of Adulthood	9
2	Adulthood, Individualization, and the Life Course	28
3	Adulthood and Social Recognition	51
4	From Adulthood as a Goal to Youth as a Value	66
5	New Adult Voices I The Meaning of Adulthood	83
6	New Adult Voices II Without a Center that Holds	98
7	Conclusion Redefining Adulthood	112
	Epilogue	119
	Notes	121
	Bibliography	125
	Index	137

PREFACE

Peter Beilharz

The new individualism presents itself to us as a serious problem, and challenge. The main reason for this is obvious. There does seem to be a weakening of ties, a corrosion of loyalty, an acceleration of time, an increasing emphasis on looking out for number one. Sometimes this care still extends to looking after a family, but now the idea of the family is also increasingly uncertain, open to dissolution and renewal. If I can make my family anew, at short notice, then there is really only me, the individual, as a core unit or reality.

Leading intellectual trends such as communitarianism and critical theory have staked a claim to blowing the whistle on these trends. They have long identified surplus individualism, or narcissism, as a major problem in the West. Perhaps this was best brought out into the sixties, by the me-generation and its chronic self-absorption, self-obsession. This line of criticism was confirmed by writers like Lasch and Sennett in the US, and later by Bauman in Europe. Here the markers are apparent. There seems to be a loss of telos, or project, for many ordinary citizens in everyday life. The moment becomes all consuming, and immediate gratification becomes overwhelming. Huxley warned us about this is *Brave New World* in 1932 already. Changed conceptions of time would lead to reduced or diminished social commitments. Prolonged adolescence would bring with it postponed adulthood. Nobody seems to want to grow up any more, especially not the young.

Yet we behave like children, us adults too. Perhaps it is rather the case that the me-generation never stopped, just kept expanding. From a properly sociological perspective, it now seems that there was a Golden Age life course—a pattern of habits and expectations unique to the period of the postwar boom. Here there was a standard life-course, standardized expectations for men, women, and children, one size fits all, and these senses expanded conceptually until we had normalized them. Certainly one historically unique aspect of the postwar period was the expansion of youth and youth culture; and this is why we need today to match the idea of new individualism with that of new adults.

Communitarianism and critical theory are always open to the criticism of nostalgia, and this indeed is legitimate. For these are intellectual traditions whose purpose is the critique of modernity, and with it the critique of the idea of progress. Yet constant vigilance is also called for here; we cannot simply presume that it was always better in the past, and in fact most of us do not believe this in terms of our everyday sensibilities and dispositions.

Harry Blatterer's contribution in this book is brilliantly to work this interface between radical critique of the present and affirmation of its actually existing contents. This brilliant book is an invitation to contemplation and conversation, not least between us, close to middle age, and our children, our students. It is elegant, beautifully written, engaging, reflexive, an exemplary sociology of everyday life.

Blatterer starts from the premise that adulthood is an invisible concept, or norm, like whiteness. We know that "maturity" is difficult, not least in the academy, or anywhere where academic professionalization means that the prospect of autonomy or recognition comes late. Youth is a brilliant theme, deeply connected to romanticism and to Enlightenment.

Do we ever grow up? We do not grow, perhaps; we learn (perhaps). We struggle, and it is this that makes us what we are. The image of standard adulthood is nevertheless normalized after World War II, after the postwar boom. This is a symptom of Fordism, set roles, Levittown, or Elizabeth in Adelaide or any new suburbs in Australia or anywhere else in the suburban world—malls rule. Fordism is then frozen as a successful normative regime; but the world keeps moving. The notion of telos or transition is arguably normalized earlier, but it is less transition than movement which is fundamental. The norm of adulthood therefore corresponds to high modernity, or in theory to modernization theory. The problem now is not that society is postmodern, but rather that it is truly modern, i.e. innerly and always mobile. Here it is the presently dominant generation—us—which is transitional. Our children are ahead of us. Our children are therefore more modern than us, who are fixed to solid modern claims. They are therefore more challenged than us by the necessity and difficulty of choice. For them, the challenge is even harder—the image of society and subject without limits, including self limits, the simultaneous sense that I can and should be everything and yet that all this is elusive.

In all this, this book is neatly and powerfully sociological; the point is not that our children are lost, it is that if we were now in our twenties, we would respond to this world in the same ways as them. The process of change, contrary to public and scholarly misconception, is therefore both historical and sociological, rather than generational. The new "generation" is a carrier, as much as a leader (or follower). Nevertheless, the image of the biography, path, *Lebenslauf* pervades even in a postvocational society. Sociologically speaking, we are plainly not only after Weber, but also after Habermas.

The power and precision of insight involved in all this is incredible, as abundantly manifest not least in the case studies developed and so well interpreted here. In fact, the book gets better as it proceeds. Adulthood is now reconsidered as personhood, and we step to recognition. The maturity and balance here is remarkable, calm, reflective, but poignant. Then we turn to youth (and implicitly to beauty, to narcissism). The analysis of paths of youth and class are brilliant. Enter the teen, the rebel, the counterculture. Now the judgement becomes wise, "be young until you die," youth as the ideology for life. This affects all of us, aging hippies no less than others.

As with Shakespeare, or Goffman, we are all players, but we are also planners. The discussion of problems of planning here is acute; the project of planning is implicitly radicalized, but we do still plan, even if we allow things to fall into place, accidentally as Heller would say, only later taking on coherence (or not; or necessity). Anyway, whatever Blatterer's interviewees say, they seem to cope; they might cope better than us. We face the two lifeworlds—theirs and ours are more connected than before; we also need to learn from them. The contemporary sense of crisis might really be ours, not theirs.

This is the core of Harry Blatterer's great achievement: to work the critical traditions which precede us against the energy, enthusiasm, and openness of these new adults who also need to negotiate the difference between their constraints and their dreams. The wonders of everyday life still precede us.

Acknowledgements

I am indebted to those from whom I have sought assistance and advice over the years. Maria Markus has been the principal guide during my own intellectual coming of age. It was a privilege and a pleasure to be her student, and she continues to be a source of inspiration in matters of scholarship as well as everyday life. Mira Crouch never let me doubt her belief in this project; she provided invaluable insights and assistance on the way. My thanks go to Clive Kessler, Jocelyn Pixley, and Michael Pusey, for their advice, support, and mentorship. Monika Ciolek's editorial assistance on an early draft was priceless, as were Norbert Ebert and Ben Mudaliar's critiques and thoughtful contributions. I am indebted to Peter Beilharz, Axel Honneth, and Kevin McDonald for their productive comments on a version of the manuscript. I thank Berghahn Books for their assistance and an anonymous reviewer for timely advice. Although I can do but scant justice to the richness of their accounts, my gratitude goes to the respondents for so freely and generously opening windows into their lives.

The love my parents and siblings show to one another and to me so unambiguously, sincerely, uncompromised by geographical distance, is the source of my perseverance. And finally: as I am approaching another threshold, which like few others is entrenched in the social imagination as a transition to adulthood, my affectionate thanks go to Aileen Woo.

Introduction

Exploring Adulthood

$\approx$❧$\approx$

Working nine to five, dinner parties, jury duty, and voting; marriages, mortgages, and children; the family sedan, adultery, and divorce; investment portfolios, nest eggs, life insurance, writing a will—these are things we do, strive for or object to, hold dear, or consider commonplace. None of these words are associated with childhood or adolescence; all of them connote in one way or another the responsibilities, commitments, and autonomy of adulthood. And just as these words describe ordinary possessions, practices, and relationships, so adulthood too has something less than remarkable about it. In fact, for most people today who consider themselves grown up, adulthood is no mystery. For them, it is the middle period of life that follows adolescence. Consequently, the need to inquire into its meaning does not arise. Yet, for an increasing number of others things are less clear-cut. As soon as they reflect and ask themselves whether or not they are actually grown up, they begin to doubt and question their adulthood. These may include 29-year-olds who "still" live with their parents; 35-year-olds in tertiary education; those in their mid thirties and beyond who are not prepared to commit to a partner, let alone a family. Add to this that in today's society statements such as "kids grow up too soon these days," or "young people just won't grow up," live side by side.

The meaning of adulthood is further unsettled by the fact that modern societies do not provide definite answers as to when it begins. This is so with respect to officialdom as well as everyday life. Even a cursory glance at the Australian Bureau of Statistics (ABS)—Australia's equivalent of Britain's National Statistics and the U.S. Census—confirms that there is no official agreement as to what age marks the beginning of adulthood. Definitions and delimitations vary according to specific areas of analysis and their relevant publications. Thus the ABS differentiates between "young people (15–24)," "population 25–64," and "older persons (65+)," while at the same time referring to those under 35 as "young people" and labeling "adult" all those 15 and over (ABS 2001a; 2003; 2004a). Similarly, the U.S. Census Bureau may refer to "adult population 18+" (USCB 2004a) just as well as to "adults age 15 and over" (J. Hess 2001).

In everyday life too we may wonder what marks the beginning of adulthood. Is it the twenty-first birthday in Anglophone societies, or perhaps reaching the age of majority at 18, 19, or 21? Is it a process of development rather than crossing one threshold or another? Perhaps self-perception is the key? Or perhaps it is marriage, parenthood, work, independent living? Taken together, these uncertainties are signs that adulthood is becoming less ordinary, that it is losing its taken-for-granted status, and that as a result the meaning of adulthood is becoming increasingly ambiguous and contingent. This contingency and ambiguity invite us to explore the social realities and experiences they suffuse.

We judge our adulthood as well as that of others in reference to institutions and practices, mentalities, worldviews, and sensibilities that are quasi outside of ourselves. These "social facts," as Emile Durkheim (1966) called them, exist prior to and beyond our lives, and yet it is we who reproduce and transform them through our actions. As lay participants in everyday life we evaluate, mostly by reflex, individuals' attainment or nonattainment of adult status according to objective achievements such as stable fulltime work, stable relationships, independent living, and parenthood. That is, although we experience them as personal circumstances we usually do not personally create these benchmarks in order specifically to mark our adulthood. These benchmarks are deeply ingrained in the culture as part of a preexisting assembly of representations and achievements that denote adult status. This is also where the seeming banality of the word "adulthood" ends.

Embedded in the word are cultural semantics that—often subtly, sometimes explicitly—provide us with clues about what it means to be welcomed into society as full members. This process of acknowledgement is one of mutuality. It is neither a matter of crossing a threshold or passing a rite of passage once and for all, nor a one-way trajectory of gradual adaptation. Rather, it is a dynamic, intersubjective process of social recognition in which collectivities and individuals are inescapably implicated.[1] Our validation as full adults occurs in our dealings with the most removed and abstract state institutions; it shapes our experiences and subjectivities at school, at work, and in voluntary associations; and it is vital to our friendships and other intimate relationships, as well as our everyday encounters with strangers. This is important to note because according to the theory of social recognition our self-esteem and self-worth, our very humanity, hinge on the way these dynamics of recognition unfold in our lives, and how—sometimes knowingly but usually through habitual actions and learned attitudes—we negotiated their vicissitudes. This is the book's raison d'être and the crux of the argument, which it elaborates in order to highlight the social constitution and the meaning of adulthood in affluent, highly differentiated, contemporary societies.

To elaborate what is social about adulthood is not to imply, however, that adulthood is somehow foisted upon us, that we are passive recipients of an ascribed position. Through our practices we not only reproduce but also challenge and change received notions and ways of life. We are at once subject to and productive of those dynamics of social recognition that shape what it means to be an adult, whatever our self-perceptions and self-identifications may be. This is rarely acknowledged in the literature where a psychological approach prevails. Both as a critique of and a complement to the individualizing perspective, the sociological perspective evoked here enables us to illuminate and then rethink some salient contradictions and ambiguities concerning the perceptions, practices, and experiences of young adults as well as their social scientific valuations.

Adulthood and Social Science

As a discipline dedicated to analyzing and interpreting social change, sociology is well situated to investigate the ambiguities and uncertainties surrounding adulthood. It may come as a surprise, then, that although time and again sociologists have marveled at the dearth of sociological investigations of adulthood as an area in its own right, none have to date addressed it adequately. The call to do just that has been made by generations of sociologists. For instance, in 1976 the journal *Daedalus* dedicated an issue to adulthood in which its editor-in-chief, Stephen R. Graubard, expressed the following concern:

> [T]he word 'adulthood' figures rarely in the scientific literature of our time; it has none of the concreteness that attaches to terms such as 'childhood' or 'adolescence,' and indeed seems almost a catch-all cry for everything that happens to the individual human being after a specific chronological age—whether eighteen, twenty-one, or some other. . . . We are insufficiently informed about how concepts of adulthood have changed over time, about how adult behavior is culturally conditioned . . . [and thus] more substantial inquiry is called for. (1976: v)

A few years later, Neil J. Smelser (1980: 2) observed: "Why the adult years, arguably the most productive and in some ways the most gratifying years in the life course, should have gone unattended for so long is a mystery." More recently, Jane Pilcher (1995: 82) echoed Smelser's sentiments when she referred to "the neglect of adulthood as a social category," as did James E. Côté (2000: 53) when he noted, "although adulthood . . . constitutes the longest period of the life course, it is the least understood." Returning to the topic in 2003, Pilcher and colleagues (2003: 1) summarized the state of affairs concerning adulthood in sociology: "It seems odd that while sociology is largely concerned with the practices and experiences of adults, there is as yet no convincing 'sociology of adulthood' equivalent to the established areas of sociologies of childhood, of youth and of old age. Moreover, each of these major stages of the life course is defined, in cultural practices and in sociological theories, largely in relation to adulthood." This book not only addresses the unusual relationship between sociology and adulthood, but also aims to make a contribution to a much-needed sociological turn, particularly in all those areas that are concerned with the life course.

Psychology, on the other hand, abounds with literature on adulthood. From the viewpoint of developmental psychology, adult individuals are expected to have made the vital decisions that give them a direction in life; to have acquired a set of stable preferences, life-guiding principles, and a range of social competencies facilitating their social interactions. Terms such as independence, responsibility for self and others, commitment, and maturity come to mind. Stability in and commitment to work and intimate relationships—"the capacity to work and love," as Freud allegedly called it—are other related criteria that are central to psychological approaches to adulthood.[2] Psychologists began to take a particular interest in this "life stage" some time after the discovery of the "midlife crisis." With this term Elliot Jacques (1965) attempted to explain a perceived rupture with earlier modalities of adulthood, although it took some ten years before the midlife crisis entered the vernacular with the publication of Gail Sheehy's *Passages* (1976). Since then there has been no shortage of psychological writings on the midlife period (e.g., B.L. Neugarten 1964; Kimmel 1974; Bischof 1976; Gould 1978; Colarusso and Nemiroff 1981; Allman 1982; Stevens-Long 1988; Commons et al. 1989; Turner and Helms 1989). In fact, the psychological approach to adulthood dominates the social scientific purview and is the main influence on sociologists dealing with the subject. In the few relevant works with a sociological bent—particularly in recent writing—adulthood is seen as dependent on individuals' self-understanding or is conceived as primarily a psychological state. By and large, these views are underpinned by a longstanding belief that adulthood lies at the end of a journey of basic psychosocial development and identity formation. As this book shows, there are historical reasons for the dominance of this view. What is of particular interest is the fact that sociologists still use this conventional, teleological model of adulthood as the template for the evaluation of young people's practices and orientations. When social trends, such as prolonged stays in the parental home, relatively late or forfeited marriage and family formation, and short-term goals are compared with this template, the conclusion is a fait accompli: an increasing number of individuals take longer to reach adulthood than was the case for previous generations. This is the standard view; it spans more than a half-century of social science discourse on the young generation and is, I suspect, not easily dislodged from its settled position. Often social scientists evaluate the trends negatively. What they perceive as particularly problematic is the transition to adulthood, rather than the nature of this presumed destination. That is to say, as far as adulthood is the focus of sociological analysis at all, it is its alleged postponement that overwhelmingly attracts attention. The meaning of adulthood remains by and large unarticulated. As a consequence, the possibility that what is understood to lie at journey's end is itself undergoing profound changes is rarely vetted.

Discourse in the media does no better. Although young people's alleged refusal to grow up is high on the agenda, reports rarely proffer opinions that go beyond a generation's supposed attitudes and consumer behavior. A good measure of cross-fertilization between social-scientific and media views ensures the reproduction of everyday assumptions about what adulthood is, and what adults ought to do or refrain from doing. As such, adulthood is a salient example of the resilience of ideas, not least because social scientists and commentators cling to their understanding of what it means to be an adult—something that is in all probability connected to their own, historically contingent experiences of growing up. But of course meanings do change, even if they change slowly: "In the course of . . . evolutionary transformations, word forms, set phrases, adages and precepts may very well continue to be handed down over the generations; however, their meaning changes and with it the way in which they pinpoint a specific referent, encapsulate specific experiences and open up new perspectives" (Luhmann 1986: 8). I trace the shifts in the meaning of a word by focusing attention on the practices and perceptions that underpin its social manifestations.

Approach and Method

I explore ways in which adulthood can be adequately conceptualized against the background of current forms of social life. I do not argue against psychologically oriented approaches, but seek to draw attention to the need for a complementary, sociological perspective from which social trends can be viewed in a larger context, and in a different light. To this end, my approach is to consider modalities of social integration in a time of advanced individualization and to reveal the affinities between culture and individuals' practices. Because little has been written about adulthood from a social-theoretical perspective, this study is skewed toward theory building. But even where the book is at its most abstract and ostensibly at considerable distance from social reality, its questions and considerations are always cast against the background of lived experience. It thus pays attention to the principal protagonists—"new adults"—throughout.[3] That is, even though their voices are heard in two specific chapters only, the active progenitors of change are present from the first page to the last. This fact, I hope, makes for good theory and thus also for good reading.

My interpretation of qualitative data is the result of conversations with twelve individuals. These conversations do not aim at the kind of scope that representative, enumerative studies may provide, but at depth (Crouch and McKenzie 2006). That is to say, I seek to identify perceptions, experiences, and attitudes in order to gain insights into contemporary adulthood as lived experience. The respondents' stories are invaluable guideposts toward a better understanding of a research area particularly when, as in the present case, that area is relatively underexplored. One of the very valuable aspects to "the logic of small samples in qualitative research" is that earlier conversations remain present as a frame of reference while new material is being offered, allowing a continuous revisiting of one interview interpretation against others (Crouch and McKenzie 2006). And so, taken together, juxtaposed against one another, and projected against a conceptual background assembled through an intensive study of relevant scholarly and nonacademic materials, thematic strands emerge that help give shape to a picture of adulthood that challenges commonsense assumptions. As a theory-building project the book investigates emerging social trends rather than analyzing specific social situations in a given milieu.

The history I sketch, and from which I draw, is the history of economically advanced, pluralist, secular societies that share the liberal-democratic tradition. The adage "Western" is thus no more than a summary concept. In fact, many of the social trends discussed here are also social realities in societies that fall outside the boundaries of what is commonly understood by the term. If not on a nationwide basis, this nevertheless pertains to more affluent milieus inside less developed or developing countries. In light of current globalizing tendencies, Eduardo Galeano's (2000: 26) distinction of "global North" and "global South" is apposite here—and points to further research possibilities. My writing about the decades following the Second World War—the time when the common-sense model of adulthood came into its own—is in no way intended as a comprehensive, differentiated exegesis of the social conditions that framed growing up during that time. This would unnecessarily stretch the limits of this volume as well as the conceptual apparatus required to reveal the emerging redefinition of adulthood. Rather, I selectively highlight some widely researched key themes that lend themselves well to comparison.

Australia is where the research is situated; its social, political, and economic conditions frame the perceptions, views, and experiences of the interviewees and thus the conceptual innovations of the text as a whole. Yet, there are benefits to an international readership that flow from this very fact. The U.S. reader will be reminded of some salient national similarities: both Australia and the U.S. are relatively new settler societies; they are part of the same linguistic community; and they share the Common Law heritage of their respective justice systems. Further, having gone through thoroughgoing economic reforms from about the middle of the 1980s, Australia is, today, firmly in the grip of a neoliberal dispensation. Under the leadership of John Howard the country has moved ever closer to the U.S. in matters of environmental, economic, and foreign policy. Like many North Americans, many Australians are familiar with the "dark side of economic reform" (Pusey 2003), just as they are familiar with terrorism's real and imagined threats. The uncertainties with which this book deals have clear—and for that reason not always articulated—links to changes in the sociopolitical environment. For example, at the time of writing, the Australian Industrial Relations system is at the brink of a transformation that could well further undermine working people's ability to envisage a coherent, long-term biographical trajectory. This particularly affects young people. U.S. citizens are no strangers to these issues, and some Europeans would do well to learn advance lessons before their governments too embark on further economic deregulation, privatization, and the inexorable, near-total individualization of all of life's responsibilities. In other words, Australia is both a typical and an extraordinary case, and as such it is well placed to give clues to an increasingly global redefinition of contemporary adulthood.

Structure of the Book

The volume proceeds from the discussion of general, conceptual questions to an exploration of personal experiences. How is adulthood culturally represented? What is the productive connection between our commonsense understanding of adulthood and its social scientific representations? What is the relationship between age norms, notions of maturity, and adulthood? How is the prevailing model of adulthood deployed in current perspectives on contemporary young adults, and how is it reproduced? These are some of the questions addressed in chapter 1. Their elaboration leads to a critique of a current orthodoxy, which I term the "delayed adulthood thesis." It examines the image of adulthood this approach uses, and by situating it in its historical context sets the scene for an alternative conceptualization developed in subsequent chapters.

The burdens as well as the opportunities of choosing from a plethora of seemingly proliferating options in what has been called "individualized society" (Bauman 2001a) and the imperative to turn one's life into a project are central moments of contemporary modernity which affect the transformation of adulthood. Chapter 2 shows that negotiating these contingencies means, in practice, to negotiate some fundamental shifts in the contemporary life course. Biographies are losing footholds of old; temporal guarantees of long standing are diminishing; uncertainty is becoming normalized, particularly for a generation that has known no different. This chapter brings into focus some of the most salient aspects of the social conditions that frame our understanding as well as the experiences of contemporary adulthood.

The following chapters are dedicated to a reconceptualization of adulthood that encompasses the social changes of the recent past as well as emerging forms of sociability. Adhering to a perspective that sees self-perception of one's adult or nonadult status as ultimately socially grounded, I elaborate this point in chapter 3 by way of Axel Honneth's theory of social recognition. Here I address our cultural association of adulthood with full personhood. This semantic cannot, however, be divorced from shifts in Western perceptions of youth—an idea that is at least as difficult to make tangible as the idea of adulthood. Youth is sometimes vaguely circumscribed as a desirable attribute, sometimes precisely delimited as a phase of life for statistical purposes. Chapter 4 discusses youth in terms of an ideology in the broad sense of the word. I trace the historical transformation and the subsequent expansion of youth as an ideal across the life course, and I connect this with dynamics of social recognition that are specific to advanced capitalist societies.

This study is an exploration of the redefinition of social norms. At the same time it is a study in social recognition. To be sure, the emergence of new norms and the changing relations of recognition are inseparable from one another. These processes unfold as a consequence of people's ordinary, everyday actions. There is perhaps no better way to illuminate changes in society than to ask those who are most directly implicated in these changes. Thus, chapters 5 and 6 turn to the experience of contemporary adulthood. I analyze material gathered in interviews in order to fathom how the respondents configure their adulthood today; how they negotiate a fragmented life course; how they deal with an all-pervasive uncertainty. By way of summary, I conclude with reflections concerning the affinities between social conditions and contemporary adulthood in the final chapter.

To seek to grasp the here and now—with one eye on the past and the other on the future, while the present shifts underfoot—is something that by its very nature can never be completely mastered. In this endeavor I have taken my lead from Zygmunt Bauman (2001a: 13), who reminds us that "close engagement with the ongoing effort to rearticulate the changing human condition under which the 'increasingly individualized individuals' find themselves as they struggle to invest sense and purpose in their lives is . . . the paramount task of sociology." This, then, is an effort to do justice to that vision and to the promise it contains.

REPRESENTATIONS OF ADULTHOOD

"What is called the common-sense view is actually the grown-up view taken for granted."

Peter Berger, *An Invitation to Sociology* (1963)

Bent on proving the value and validity of sociology as a scientific discipline, and critiquing the psychology of his day to make his point, Emile Durkheim used the term "collective representations" to describe the social a priori of ideas. Relatively fixed, even time honored, myths, legends, religious beliefs, and moral sentiments have in Durkheim's conception a strongly constraining and integrating function. Taking his lead from the venerable pioneer, contemporary French social psychologist Serge Moscovici has coined the term "social representations." In *La Psychoanalyse, son image et son public* he offers this explanation:

> Social representations are almost tangible entities. They circulate, intersect and crystallize continuously, through a word, a gesture, or a meeting in our daily world. They impregnate most of our established social relations, the objects we produce or consume, and the communications we exchange. We know that they correspond, on one hand, to the symbolic substance which enters into their elaboration, and on the other to the practice which produces this substance, much as science or myth corresponds to a scientific or mythical practice. (quoted in Duveen 2000: 3)

Unlike Durkheim's collective representations, which appear like an impenetrable layer of sundry sentiments, emotions, and beliefs, Moscovici emphasizes the mutability and plasticity of commonly held ideas, not least because social representations are intersubjectively constituted through verbal and nonverbal communication. In turn, as embodiments of our collectively held ideas, they orient our practices. Not unlike Durkheim's (1966) axiom that social facts are things *sui generis*, Moscovici proposes, "to consider as a *phenomenon* what was previously seen as a *concept*" (2000: 30, original emphasis). It is in Moscovici's sense that adulthood can be usefully considered a social representation.

Adulthood is circumscribed by historically and culturally specific practices and expectations, achievements, and competencies. It is fixed in our minds as childhood's other, and as adolescence's not-yet-attained destination. More than a concept, and testimony to the power of ideas, this social representation enacts differences: the child and adolescent are cast as dependent on adults. To better grasp adulthood as a social representation, let us imagine that it was struck from the imagination. Beyond the nonexistence of a mere sound, a range of associated concepts and ideas would be divested of their present meaning. What are childhood and adolescence without their counterpart and goal? How would we understand maturity and autonomy? The evaluative potency of adulthood (its taken-for-granted centrality in the apportioning of power) would be missing, replaced perhaps by other concepts conjured up by collective practices and ideas. This illustrates "the curious position" of social representations "somewhere between concepts, which have as their goal abstracting meaning from the world and introducing order into it, and percepts, which reproduce the world in a meaningful way" (Moscovici 2000: 31).

As part of the social constitution of adulthood, everyday communication and social scientific discourse feed off each other and reproduce the cluster of meanings and representations with which the word adulthood has become associated over time. In fact, it is of fairly recent provenance as a word, and of even more recent pedigree as a commonsense concept and social phenomenon. Still, the meaning of ideas, concepts, and social phenomena changes along with large-scale social transformations. Today, demographic and cultural transformations that originate in the post–Second World War decades are forcing apart ideas about adulthood and the practices that produce its substance. The emerging cleavage is manifest in a *normative lag* between commonsense and social scientific discourse, and the practical redefinition of adulthood on the ground. This is a central argument of the book. Thus it is worth exploring adulthood and its emergence as a concept, its transmutation into and consolidation as a social representation, as well as the present dilemmas these changes pose for social scientists in general and sociologists in particular. On the whole this task has a twofold aim: to elucidate the interaction between commonsense and social scientific knowledge in the formation of our cultural vision of adulthood, and to address how this conception is used in approaches to new adults' practices and orientations.

A Brief History of Adulthood and Maturity

The word adulthood, denoting a stage of life, is a relatively recent addition to the English lexicon. According to the *Oxford English Dictionary*, usage of the noun was preceded by the adjective "adult," which entered the vocabulary via the adoption of the French *adulte*, itself a sixteenth-century adaptation of the Latin *adolescere*, to grow up. "Adultness" is said to have come into usage mid-eighteenth-century, and was superseded around 1870 by "adulthood." The Shakespearian scholar Charles Cowden Clarke (1787–1877) is credited with using the term for the first time in a literary work. Writing about Shakespeare's *Twelfth Night*, he noted that the play "was written in the full vigour and adulthood of his [Shakespeare's] conformation" (OED 1989: 178–180).

Some time passed, however, before the social meaning of adulthood was to gain normative efficacy. Preindustrial Western cultures did not know adulthood as a defined social category: "You were a man or a woman if you weren't a child" (Merser 1987: 52). In the United States the term came into circulation after the Civil War and reached prominence no sooner than the early twentieth century. Winthrop Jordan (1978) stresses that this was linked to the increasing fashionableness of the notion of psychological maturity, which at that time began to develop into a metaphor for adult status. Jordan identifies as crucial to the emergence of the mature individual qua adult the transformation of Calvinist predestinarianism into a theology that emphasized individual effort as the means to salvation: "Only when the individual's own struggles were given far greater weight in the process of conversion would there be room for a process of reaching psychological maturity" (1978: 190). So, the emergence of adulthood is inextricably linked to processes of individualization, that is, individuals' gradual liberation from the determinants of birth and religious conformity, and their simultaneous charging with an ever-increasing self-responsibility for all aspects of their lives.

Toward the end of the nineteenth and the beginning of the twentieth century adulthood became the default position: a life stage situated between adolescence and old age. G. Stanley Hall's (1904) work on adolescence was pivotal in this regard. Hall's thought was influenced by post-Darwinian evolutionary biology. His work was an important precursor to developmental psychology, which, particularly in its early to mid-twentieth-century form, set about segmenting the life course into discrete and well-defined units. It followed that adolescence, which was ever more perceived and treated as a period of inner turmoil, came to denote a preparatory life stage to adulthood, now understood as its developmental goal.

Earlier, in preindustrial Europe for example, children took on adult responsibilities at a young age by today's standards. For some sectors of society at least, participation in productive work tended to extend across almost all of the life span. Furthermore, the combination of early family formation, short life expectancy, and high fertility rates meant that parenthood too was a lifelong endeavor for most. As Hareven (1978: 205) puts it, "demographic, social and cultural factors combined to produce only minimal differentiation in the stages of life." Moreover, the separation of young people from the world of production through universal education, while exclusion from work was also replicated at the other end of the life course, played an important role in the emergence of adulthood as a separately conceived life phase (Pilcher 1995).

Adulthood emerged in public consciousness and entered the cultural vocabulary of everyday life as the achievable (and indeed desirable) end to adolescent immaturity during the Second World War. In the U.S. a fascination with being grown up emerged in popular culture. *Reader's Digest, McCall's,* and *Vital Speeches of the Day* were some of the publications with a wide readership that concerned themselves with what it meant to be adult. A 1952 issue of *Reader's Digest,* for example, invited young readers to complete a quiz in order to find out whether or not they were indeed grown up (Jordan 1978: 197). So, since its entry into the vernacular during the Civil War, adulthood had come to signify something solid to aim for, a life stage that held the promise of fulfilled wishes and achieved aspirations. Accordingly, a number of words, phrases, and practices associated with adulthood as social status began to settle and eventually became taken for granted and commonplace. Directives like "Don't be childish!" and "Grow up!" and turns of phrase such as being "set in your ways" or having "settled down," are linguistic devices associated with adulthood. They are also figures of speech that enact social asymmetries and put adult "human beings" in a more powerful position vis-à-vis those who, like children, are perceived and treated as "human becomings" (Qvortrup 1994).

"Maturity" acts as a central metaphor encompassing normative achievements and attributes of adulthood. Although the term is most closely associated with biological development, maturity tends to be used to describe individuals' social and psychological competencies and dispositions. While being mature does not necessarily make a person an adult in the eyes of others (a child may be "mature for her age," just as an adult may be deemed immature), when linked to adulthood, maturity denotes an end state to biological, psychological, and social development. The notion of social maturity adds an extra dimension. It takes as its starting point the premise that adulthood is constituted not so much by the significance individuals attribute to their own attitudes and actions, but by the kinds of social validation these attract. Just as the interpretation of biological and psychological maturity is culturally specific, as Margaret Mead's classic work *Coming of Age in Samoa* (1928) has shown, maturity is subject to socially constructed and acknowledged forms of meaning. Its plural meanings (biological, psychological, and social) are, for example, institutionalized in law. To appropriate the thinking behind James and Prout's (1997) social constructivist stance on childhood: the maturity of adults is a biological fact of life, but the ways in which this maturity is understood and made meaningful is a fact of culture.[1]

Notions of maturity hold an important place in the self-understanding of entire societies that share the liberal European tradition. The obvious example here is Immanuel Kant's (1724–1804) statement, "Enlightenment is humankind's emergence from self-incurred immaturity" (1975 [1784]). In his critical analysis of this text, Michel Foucault spells out the synonymy between history and individual development. He maintains that Kant defines the historical process "as humanity's passage to its adult status," to "maturity" (1994: 308–9, 318). Similarly, historian Norman Davies comments, "Europeans reached the 'age of discretion' . . . with medieval Christendom seen as the parent and Europe's secular culture as a growing child conceived in the Renaissance" (Davies 1996: 596). Common perspectives of human development from a state of childlike dependence to adult independence parallel our understanding of modernization as a process of emancipation from dogma, tradition, and authority. This direct link between historical process and individual maturation has consequences for the social-scientific appraisal and treatment of young people to this day. The clearest case, again, is Hall's early interpretation of adolescence, where the individual's development was said to recapitulate the historical maturation of the human species as a whole. Along with a new emphasis on personal and social development, certain practices emerged as symbolic and constitutive of adulthood.

Adult Practices

Picture this: a man and a woman in their mid-twenties. The woman holds a baby in her arms; a small child clings to the man's hand. The woman wears an apron, the man his work overalls. A "Sold" sign perches on the fence that surrounds the freshly painted house. A generously sized car sits in the driveway. No one could ever mistake the man and woman in this romanticized picture for adolescents, and few would be tempted to suggest that they were not adults. Many would, as if by reflex, assume the man to be husband to the woman and father to the child. But something about this image jars against the present. Just like the choice of frame for a painting or a photo, so the right time frame too helps integrate representation and reception. With this in mind, I suggest that no period in the history of Western societies has been more conducive to the institutionalization of a particular model of adulthood (of which the above, romanticized image is one possible representation) than the era historian Eric Hobsbawm (1995) has called the "Golden Age," namely the time between the end of the Second World War and the oil crises of the early 1970s. No period has provided more favorable conditions for this model to become lived experience for a majority; no period has shown a more faultless synthesis of ideal and reality. Following Lee (2001), I call this synthetic construct "standard adulthood."

After the Second World War the industrialized economies experienced unprecedented affluence and stability. The period from about 1945 to the early

1970s saw a concerted effort by business, government, and unions to prevent a recurrence of the Depression, the harrowing experience of which still haunted decision makers. Although more wealthy nations had their own macroeconomic agenda, public spending, full employment, and universal social security provisions were given priority to ensure internal demand and hence economic expansion. The then-prevailing mode of management and organization, what came to be known as Fordism, has since come to denote more than that: it signifies a once-prevalent "total way of life" that congealed around goals of long-term stability and economic growth (Harvey 1989: 135). Typically, businesses valued employee loyalty, which was generally rewarded with promotions in hierarchically constituted organizations. For employees and families this meant that there were plannable career paths with predictable milestones on the way, and a known destination: retirement on guaranteed government pensions. In the world of work the accumulation of experience with age was viewed as a valuable asset and was seen to increase, rather than inhibit, job security (Lee 2001: 11–13). According to one sociologist's interpretation of the time—characteristically exaggerated for illustrative purposes—these economic and work-related aspects alone, "created a society in which people's lives were as highly standardized as the sheet steel from which the cars were welded together" (Beck 2000: 68).

These social conditions corresponded to a value system that remained unchallenged in its normative validity until the rising discontent of the 1960s. Open same-sex relationships were extremely risqué and hence rare, and same-sex parenthood (as opposed to guardianship) was unimaginable. The heterosexual nuclear family prevailed as the ideal. It is during this time that early marriage and family formation came to be lived experience for many adults.[2] Add to this the opportunities provided by the labor market, and a picture emerges that one commentator draws with clarity:

> [O]nce 'adult' and employed, one could expect to stay 'the same' for the rest of one's life in a range of ways; one's identity was stabilized by sharing the work environment with more or less the same people throughout one's working life; the geographical area one lived in would remain the same since the organization one belonged to had set down firm roots in that area; and, even if one were dissatisfied with one's job, one would not have to seek a position with another organization (in another place with different people) because time and effort would bring the reward of career progression. (Lee 2001: 12–13)

Flexibility—first a buzzword in the New Capitalism (Sennett 1998, 2006) and now a taken for granted imperative in all social relations—was as yet a far-off reality. Becoming adult was a matter of following a life course that resembled a veritable march through the institutions of marriage, parenthood, and work. By today's standards these objective markers of adulthood were relatively fixed, achievable, and supported by an overarching value consensus. There was a high degree of fit between norms and social practice. Sharply delineated structures of opportunity rested on culturally and socially reproduced normative foundations that were, for a time, rarely questioned. With fulltime long-term work within reach for a majority, and with early marriage and family formation so common, what being grown up meant was clear. The fulfillment of the *classic markers of adulthood* (family, stable relationships, work, and independent living) brought in its wake the social recognition necessary for adult status to become a meaningful achievement. The experience of affluence and stability after the Second World War thus added its share of securities to the vision of standard adulthood, a now crystallized social representation.

Not all was well in the Golden Age, however. For one, growing up as a member of the postwar generation in the West was to live a contradiction. The Cold War meant that the new reality of increased chances for social mobility and relative affluence, and the belief in continuing economic and technological advance, was checked by the knowledge that the possibility of total annihilation was just as real. For example, the Cuban Missile Crisis of 1962 served as a stark reminder of tragic possibilities.[3] The lived contradiction of threat and opportunity underpinned one of the so-called "baby boomer" generation's defining mottos: "We're not here for a long time, we're here for a good time" (Mackay 1997: 62). As we shall see in chapter 4, this attitude marks an ideological transformation in the meaning of youth that was to reverberate decades into the future and that significantly altered the meaning of adulthood.

My schematic equation—economic stability plus an explicitly sanctioned normative consensus equals a stable adult identity—is not intended to be positive nostalgia.[4] After all, standard adulthood was highly gendered in an era when the labor market overwhelmingly favored men as breadwinners. It would also be a gross historical misrepresentation were this image to be generalized to include marginalized groups. The kind of stability and predictability of life suggested by this model of adulthood is based primarily upon the experiences of white, heterosexual, middle-class males; on experiences, that is, that were lived in mainstream families and reproduced in mainstream culture, whatever the extant inequalities. The crux of the matter is this: the real differences did not diminish standard adulthood's *normative* status as the ultimate benchmark for adult maturity. Our contemporary associations of adulthood with stability arose from that generation's experiences and expectations.

Today standard adulthood as a norm remains robust, though it may be increasingly counterfactual for many. It is still associated with the ideals of stable relationships, stable work and income, a family of one's own, and independent living (Furstenberg et al. 2003; 2004). Framed in the language of a specific kind of maturity, standard adulthood promises greater self-understanding and the self-confidence that comes with the accumulation of social competencies. In these terms, settling down is not to be shunned. When the experience of opportunity, possibility, and stability is passed from one generation to the next and is focused in a notion such as adulthood, it stands to reason that this cultural idea should become a powerful ideal.

Classic Markers of Adulthood

The achievement of adult status has to do with "sets of practical accomplishments, and repertoires of behaviour" (Pilcher 1995: 86). This is particularly necessary in modern societies due to the absence of all-encompassing, firmly instituted rites of passage to adulthood. Thus there are various signposts that serve to identify and acknowledge individuals as adults, such as age, independent living, stable relationships, parenthood, stable employment, and the right to vote, to name a few. The descriptors of adulthood discussed below are limited to those objective markers of adulthood that have long standing salience as achievements that are deeply embedded in dynamics of social recognition. As ideal-typical yardsticks for commonsense and social scientific judgments regarding individuals' status, these classic markers are the tangibles of standard adulthood.

Marriage with its ritualistic inauguration is one such instance. It is ingrained in the social imaginary and as such most closely approximates a transition ritual from adolescence to adulthood. Through marriage people enter into a union underwritten by a tacit understanding that *responsibility* and *commitment*, central notions in the cultural vocabulary of adulthood, are vital ingredients for its success. The institution of marriage and adult status are linked through the symbolism of the wedding ring. This badge of membership in the world of adults can be a sign of integrity; it can signify a shared fate; it can spell "off limits" as well as "discretion assured." Above all, it symbolizes an act of commitment, its diminishing chances of survival notwithstanding.[5] Marriage evinces the overcoming of reputed youthful self-absorption and hedonism. In everyday life it connotes the achievement of adulthood anchored in commitment and responsibility to someone (spouse) and something (a stable relationship).

As Eisenstadt (1971: 30) maintains, adult status "coincides with the transition period from the family of orientation to that of procreation, as it is through this transition that the definite change of age roles, from receiver to transmitter of cultural tradition, from child to parent, is effected." The social validation attained through *parenthood* is palpable in everyday interaction. Outings with children often involve conversations with strangers, previously perhaps a rarity. In the supermarket, at the bus stop, in the park; there always appears to be someone willing to share their experiences, wanting a peek at your baby, encouraging or reprimanding your particular style of child rearing, commenting on the difficulties of work/life balance. To paraphrase a respondent (with sociological training) in my sample who had recently been "catapulted" into twin fatherhood, this is "social integration at its most intimate." Particularly in the post–Second World War era, adulthood and family life were inextricably bound together in the social imagination. As Furstenberg et al. (2004: 35) put it with reference to the United States: "By the 1950s and 1960s, most Americans viewed family roles and adult responsibilities as nearly synonymous. In that era, most women married before they were 21 and had at least one child before they were 23. For men, having the means to marry and support a family was the defining characteristic of adulthood, while for women, merely getting married and becoming a mother conferred adult status."

Many of us remember the question "what do you want to be when you grow up?" when "be" really meant "do." *Work*—showing that you are capable of "paying your own way," "pulling your weight," contributing to the family and to society independently of state or parents—is another commonsense marker of adulthood. Stock phrases such as "wait 'til you're out in the real world" and "welcome to the real world" are historically framed. Since the completion of the process of differentiation that assigned children their place in school and adults their place in work (Gillis 1981; Mitterauer 1992; Perrot 1997), adulthood is also partly defined by independence gained through participation in the "work society" (Offe 1984).

Independence from parents is most explicitly achieved with the realization of *independent living*. To this end, leaving home has long been an integral part of one's identification as an autonomous individual, because "for much of the twentieth century, home-leaving was the starting point for a range of processes that signaled the transition from youth to adulthood. Most young people left home to marry, complete their education, serve in the military, or to work. With those changes came parenthood and economic independence" (Pullum et al. 2002: 555). In Australia home ownership is part of the national imaginary; it is a dream to be made reality through hard work and frugality. A stable relationship, parenthood, and work can thus be seen as finding their culmination in the family home as the meaning-giving reference point. The key to the home—just like the key to the parental home some receive at their twenty-first birthday in Anglophone societies—also opens the door to the world of adults.

These classic markers of adulthood provide the social frame for standard adulthood, a model that not only approximates many contemporary adults' lives, but that is the normative model par excellence. Although these are by no means all the characteristics that are attributable to adulthood, they are central cultural typifications and as such impact on public opinion just as much as on social research.

Adulthood and Age

The social constitution of adulthood can be further clarified by considering the rift between social practice and biological factors. In the course of Western history the onset of puberty has been slowly but steadily occurring at ever-younger ages (Mitterauer 1992). This does not mean, however, that Western societies, in contrast to some other cultures, accept the attained physical ability to procreate as marking the transition to adulthood. Rather, it is the social actualization of a physiological capacity through parenthood that has, historically speaking, marked this transition. To make matters more intricate still, the timing of such an event, measured against culturally specific and more or less institutionalized age norms, plays a pivotal role. Thus, in the absence of explicit rites of passage, one immediate problem in contemporary society is the lack of empirical determinacy as to when adulthood begins. This is paradoxical insofar as the life course is to a significant degree rationalized along age lines (Buchmann 1989; Settersten 2003).[6] The age-structured pathway through primary and secondary education is an obvious example. Yet, the search for a definitive point at which adulthood is formally marked as beginning is futile.

Age legislation is a case in point. The law adheres to a pluralist conception of maturity denoting various competencies that are distributed among a range of ages. Thus, entry into adulthood is conceived in extraordinarily fragmented terms. For instance, depending on the age difference between partners, sexual preferences, and state legislation, the age of consent ranges from 14 to 18 in the United States and from 10 to 18 in Australia. The age of criminal responsibility in the U.S. is as low as 7 depending on state legislature (not all states specify minimum ages) (CNIJ 1997). In Australia it is 10, while in other countries it is 14 (Austria, Germany), 16 (Japan, Spain) or 18 years of age (Belgium, Luxembourg) (Urbas 2000; AIC 2003).[7] A variety of other acts are deemed legal at different ages. In Australia, movies rated "M" for mature may be viewed from age 15, the same age at which individuals are free to leave school of their own accord. Cinema goers have to purchase full-price tickets from age 16, the age at which people can opt to get tattooed and are allowed to purchase cigarettes. At age 18 individuals are permitted to vote, carry firearms, get married, make medical decisions, and so forth (*Sunday Age* 1992; Urbas 2000; DHA 2003). This illustrates that entry to adulthood, as far as legislation is concerned, occurs on a continuum along which rights and obligations are incrementally attributed. Even if we were to speak of a legal adulthood that comes with the attainment of full legal rights and obligations at age 18, 19, or 21, this does not pertain to noncitizens regardless of age (e.g., permanent residents, prisoners, refugees, and asylum seekers). And although they are in principle, in fact individuals are neither guaranteed equal access to the law, nor protected from structural exclusion.

These official ambiguities are in tension with "informal age norms" (Settersten 2003) that function as cultural reference points to behavior and status. The relationship between age and the classic markers of adulthood is an example, for the latter depend for normative effectiveness on when in a person's life they are achieved. Stable relationships or parenthood, work or independent living attained too soon may be interpreted as signs of precociousness or devi-ance rather than adult competence. Likewise, late attainment may entail physi-cal risks (childbirth); it may be increasingly difficult (work), or deemed behind schedule (marriage, independent living). Clearly, what is regarded as late or early is historically and culturally contingent. We may also think about the sig-nificance of the twenty-first birthday in some societies, or the confidence with which individuals remark on how young or old somebody looks "for their age" without the slightest need for expert opinion. This is not to privilege informal over formal age norms on points of accuracy, however. Ageism can be institu-tionalized both in everyday interaction as well as in the official sense. Whether this pertains to discrimination against elderly individuals, or to disrespect of those who simply appear to be too young to be given credence for full adult status, age is a powerful ascriptive force in contemporary society. In fact, age norms are an exception to Parsons' (1951) rule that with modernity premodern ascription gives way to achievement, that status is now exclusively a matter of individual action rather than predetermined parameters. To the contrary, infor-mal as well as formal age norms are social facts that are culturally reproduced and shored up. They facilitate and inhibit social participation. They are mark-ers of inclusion just as much as they are points of discrimination.

We can see, then, that the practical, everyday taken-for-grantedness of adult-hood is at odds with its conceptual indeterminacy. Neither official age grading nor the attribution of rights and obligations; neither biological characteristics nor psychological traits; neither formal nor informal age norms; neither fixed roles nor rites of passage can be drawn upon to delineate and therefore define adulthood. All these aspects are in silent tension with one another, contradic-tory, imperfectly integrated. Yet, in the social imagination adulthood remains the central stage of the biography—that which childhood moves toward and which old age has left behind.

Prolonged Adolescence, Postponed Adulthood?

Media reports consistently focus on the practices of young people who according to cultural age norms ought to be grown up, but are described as at best deferring and at worst rejecting adulthood. These reports by and large attempt to come to grips with the social trends that underpin the alleged problems of contemporary young adulthood: prolonged stay in or episodic returns to the parental home; de-layed or altogether forfeited marriage and family formation; drifting from tempo-rary job to temporary job; or the repudiation of long-term aspirations in favor of short-term goals and experimental living. Some selected headlines from newspa-pers and magazines exemplify this discourse. Here, those who ask "Why Today's Teenagers are Growing up Early" (*Sydney Morning Herald* 2001a) are countered by a majority typically expressing sentiments along these lines: "Now Wait til 35 for Coming of Age" (*Australian* 2001), "'Adults' Fail the Age Test" (*Herald Sun* 2004), "Kids Who Refuse to Grow Up" (*Herald Sun* 2003), and "Forever Young Adultescents Won't Grow Up" (*MX Australia* 2004). Articles of this kind are mostly based on the claims of market researchers who believe that the "fundamental philosophy [of people in their twenties and beyond] is a deferment of any sort of commitment . . . Underpinning that is a sense of the now, and little sense of the future" (*Australian* 2004). In keeping with their arguments, and to enable them to target new consumer demographics, marketing professionals offer a number of labels describing individuals who are said to be averse to growing up. These descriptors are readily taken up in the media where there is talk about the rise of "adultescents," "kidults," and "twixters" in the U.S. and Australia, "boomerang kids" in Canada, Nesthocker in Germany, mammone in Italy, and KIPPERS (Kids In Parents' Pockets Eroding Retirement Savings) in the U.K. (*Time* 2005a; *Time* 2005b).[8]

Social scientists have evolved their own concepts to accommodate essentially the same view. Indeed, media attention to young people's deferral or rejection of adulthood can draw on expert advice with a long history. Although in reality a number of approaches differ in nuance, for analytic clarity I subsume these under the *delayed adulthood thesis*. As intimated above, twentieth-century North American notions of adolescence as a period of "structured irresponsibility" (Parsons 1942a) and as "identity crisis" (Erikson 1950) can be considered paradigmatic of Western culture's perceptions and treatment of adolescents up to the present. Taking the "storm and stress" view as a given, psychoanalyst Peter Blos (1941) coined the term "post-adolescence." It designates a stage of life inhabited by individuals who have outgrown adolescence, but have not yet reached adulthood. These are individuals who, according to Keniston (1970: 634), "far from seeking the adult prerogative of their parents . . . vehemently demand a virtually indefinite prolongation of their nonadult state." Erikson's (1968) "prolonged adolescence" neatly encapsulates this idea—a vision that continues to have currency today. What for marketers and journalists are twixters, adultescents, and kidults, for social scientists are lives led in a manner that is analogous with a particular image of adolescence: a time of irresponsibility where few decisions have to be made, and the capacity to reconcile "work and love" has not yet been completely attained. Consequently, contemporary trends are then equated with a prolonged transition to and delayed entry into full adulthood (e.g., Côté 2000; Furstenberg et al. 2003, 2004; Arnett 2004; Settersten et al. 2005; Schwartz et al. 2005).

Sociologist Frank Furedi (2003: 5) is unequivocal in his condemnation of what he perceives to be an "infantilisation of contemporary society." Taking umbrage at adults' alleged "present-day obsession with childish things"—gadgetry of all kinds, including soft toys and children's books—he asserts: "Hesitations about embracing adulthood reflect a diminished aspiration for independence, commitment and experimentation." His agreement with social psychologist Stephen Richardson, who holds that "we do not reach maturity until the age of 35" (quoted in Furedi 2003: 5), also speaks volumes about social scientists' perspective on adolescence as a time of immaturity, and adulthood as the culmination of a kind of maturity that Peter Berger (1966: 69) described as that "state of mind that has settled down, come to terms with the status quo, given up the wilder dreams of adventure and fulfillment." This kind of view, of which Furedi's essay is but one articulation, illustrates how late-nineteenth-century ideas about young people (and prevailing normative notions of masculinity and adulthood) are still deployed in social-scientific analyses of present trends. And it does so with particular eloquence because its advocates, in all their earnestness, appear entirely oblivious of this very fact. Hans Peter Duerr's (1985: 126) assertion that one of the tasks of the scientist is to "mount a defence against that which is strange," has some resonance here, if only as a possible unconscious motivation rather than full intention.

In fact, with this (unacknowledged but implied) model of adolescence in mind, proponents of the delayed adulthood thesis at times assert with some certainty when adolescence now ends and adulthood begins. Thus the U.S. National Academy of Sciences pegs the end of adolescence at 30 years of age (Danesi 2003: 104–5). The issue becomes positively confusing when, in a programmatic statement on professional confidentiality, members of the U.S. Society for Adolescent Medicine state, "[a]dolescents who are age 18 or older are adults" (Ford et al. 2004: 164). There is, in other words, no social-scientific consensus concerning the end of one period of life and the beginning of the next. There is agreement, however, that today young people take longer to reach full adulthood than was previously the case. Furstenberg (2000: 898) sums up the prevailing accord: "[T]he transition to adulthood extend[s] well into the third decade of life and is not completed by a substantial fraction of young people until their 30s."

To accommodate the demographic changes that lie at the root of the allegedly protracted and delayed entry into adulthood in affluent societies, two conceptions of North American provenance have gained particular currency: Jeffrey J. Arnett's "emerging adulthood," and "early adulthood," a concept marshaled by a MacArthur Foundation research group into transitions to adulthood headed by Frank F. Furstenberg. Both perspectives are based on the belief that a new life stage separates adolescence from adulthood. Emerging adulthood pertains to individuals between 18 and approximately 25 years of age who, "[h]aving left the dependency of childhood and adolescence, and having not yet entered the enduring responsibilities that are normative in adulthood," inhabit an in-between stage (Arnett 2000a: 469). Early adulthood describes a phase from the late teens to the late twenties or early thirties when "young people have not yet become fully adult because they are not ready or able to perform the full range of adult roles" (Furstenberg et al. 2003: 1). According to Arnett (2000a: 471), terms such as "late adolescence," "young adulthood," and by implication "early adulthood," should be avoided because emerging adults "do not see themselves as adolescents, but many of them also do not see themselves entirely as adults." The main difference between these approaches, then, is one of nomenclature. In fact, the research agendas are eminently compatible both in terms of their respective subject areas and conclusions. They are erudite elaborations of the notion that the transition to adulthood is increasingly extended, and that thus entry into full adulthood occurs later than was previously the case—that the twixters, the kidults, and adultescents are on the rise.

Taken in sum, Arnett and Furstenberg et al.'s research output makes important contributions to the study of young people's experiences and the shifting normative frame in which they unfold. Be it the chronicling of social transformations in the United States since the Second World War; be it the subjective perceptions of the transition to adulthood (Arnett 1997) and the perceptions and attitudes of young people concerning their futures (Arnett 2000b); be it North Americans' views about the timing of life events that for them connote the transition to adulthood (Furstenberg et al. 2003; 2004): the combined findings are significant contributions to our understanding of subjective views and manifestations of social changes. But the validity and utility of data hinge ultimately on how they contribute to concept building, and how new concepts are put to use. This is particularly important when we attempt to describe and understand the experiences of young people, not least because policies informed by this kind of research have a very real and direct impact on young people. For this reason alone the prevailing view needs to be expanded. A first step is to point out some inherent misconceptions, not least because they underpin much of the work done in the area of "youth transitions."

Epistemological Fallacy I: The Subjectivization of Everything

The aforementioned researchers have made invaluable contributions to our understanding of young people's perceptions of adolescence and the transition to adulthood, and perhaps none more so than Arnett. However, something is amiss in his interpretation of the data. Arnett connects what is considered a highly individualized Western culture directly to the alleged personalization of life stages. To this end the following statement may be considered programmatic not only for Arnett's approach, but for much of the oeuvre: "The more individualistic a culture becomes, the more the transition to adulthood is individually rather than socially defined. It takes place subjectively, individually, internally, in an individual's sense of having reached a state of self-sufficiency, emotional self-reliance, and behavioral self-control" (Arnett and Taber 1994: 533, original emphasis). This assertion fits hand in glove with Côté's (2000: 31) claim, "adulthood is now more a psychological state than a social status." In fact, Côté's approach to the changing nature of adulthood is instructive here, and it is worth addressing, not least because of his recent collaboration with Arnett (Schwartz et al. 2005)—a quasi-natural affiliation considering their respective approaches. Central to Côté's view on identity formation in emerging adulthood is what he calls "two developmental routes in the individualization process" (Schwartz et al. 2005). As he previously elaborated in *Arrested Adulthood* (2000), Côté distinguishes between passive "default individualization" and active "developmental individualization" in his analysis of people's orientations concerning their life trajectories.[9] Consumer-corporate interests are said to perpetuate and benefit from the default option; pop culture thrives on the illusory notion that individuality is a function of "selecting the right wardrobe or developing slight affectations in speech, behavior or appearance" (2000: 34). An increasing number of adults are seen as taking "paths of least resistance" rather than acquiring "self-discipline, in order to develop advanced skills, aptitudes, and attitudes" (2000: 34). Drawing on his notion of "identity capital," Côté suggests that individuals need to become successful investors in the identity market in order to reach their potentials despite the machinations of a media-driven pop culture.

While both Arnett and Côté have succeeded in highlighting young people's potential for agency, objections can be raised. Their focus on individual perception and individual agency/passivity psychologizes the meaning of adulthood. This renders the young people under scrutiny agents of their own fate to such an overdrawn extent that the systemic factors that influence their practices all but disappear from view, except to provide obligatory variables. Practitioners in the sociology of youth have shown that today young people are under great pressure to succeed at a time when structural adjustments have softened up the foundations on which they are to build their lives, and that they often do so believing themselves to be solely responsible for their successes and failures (Furlong and Cartmel 1997; McDonald 1999; Wyn and White 2000; Dwyer and Wyn 2001). This blindness to systemic conditions on individuals' behalf has been called "the epistemological fallacy of late modernity" (Furlong and Cartmel 1997). Precisely this fallacy is discursively reproduced and social-scientifically legitimated by the orthodox, highly individualistic approach to adulthood.

Epistemological Fallacy II: The Normative Lag

The prevailing pronouncements about young people's practices have one thing in common: they implicitly use the model of standard adulthood as their benchmark. Wagner and Hayes's (2005: 4) considerations are instructive in this regard: "Our present-day thinking is based on a succession of historically evolved mentalities; on mental edifices which previous generations have constructed, pulled down, renovated and extended. Past events are compressed in images and metaphors which determine our present thinking even if we are not always aware of them." Standard adulthood, a commonsense life stage in the "thickly viscous form of the past" (Wagner and Hayes 2005: 4), remains conceptually fixed, unproblematic, and thus escapes articulation, let alone analysis. What is seen as worthy of analysis, however, is the failure to reach a taken-for-granted standard at a time of life when this is conventionally deemed most appropriate. In fact, research into the timing of the transition to adulthood has shown that today the realization of the classic markers of adulthood is still expected by most people to occur in their twenties (Arnett 1997; Du Bois-Reymond 1998; Furstenberg et al. 2003; 2004). The nonattainment of these markers by many people in their twenties and beyond is thus taken as a sign that their adolescent state is prolonged, that they in fact defer or reject adulthood for a time, only to emerge into the standard model of adulthood later. What is most significant for now is the fact that the current benchmark of adult behavior is anachronistic. Ideal types are useful instruments in sociological methods. As is well known, Max Weber (1922) advocated their use. But proponents of the delayed adulthood thesis not only refrain from using standard adulthood as an ideal type in order to gauge present or past deviations from it, but actually confuse a historically contingent model with contemporary social realities and continue to posit the ideal type as the normative telos to individual development. What is more, the outdated model is often held up as something to be striven for at a time when the realization of standard adulthood is for many not only impossible, but also hardly desirable (e.g., Du Bois-Reymond 1998; see also chapters 5 and 6 in this volume). Social scientists, journalists, and marketers, members of the previous generation as well as young adults themselves are thus frequently subject to a normative lag between the idea of standard adulthood and contemporary realities. In the long view of history such delays are commonly recognized: "Mentalities are at any one time the most sluggish components of historical change. They lag behind . . . and establish contradictions and rogue complications in historical development . . . In this way, they become the driving force behind new change" (Wagner and Hayes 2005: 3). In our specific context, analysis of this normative lag is perhaps nowhere of greater urgency than in those policy domains that deal with young people's transition from education to work. As Peter Dwyer and Johanna Wyn (2001: 78) assert:

> Relying on our own past . . . establishes a predetermined expectation about what happens in the lives of the next generation. It takes for granted a linear model of development which assumes that young people progress through a pre-set series of separate stages in their lives which involve innate processes of maturation and normative forms of socialization within stable families and an age-based education system, leading at the proper time to a movement from dependence to independence, from school to work, from young people's status as adolescents to their eventual achievement of a stable and secure adulthood.

This illustrates the point that the normative lag also translates into a policy gap between the ideology of increased educational participation and the persistent uncertainties of outcomes for the post-1970 generation (Dwyer and Wyn 2001: 74)—a gap, that is, that takes the linearity of a previous generation's transition to adulthood as the evaluative and policy-forming benchmark by which young people's successes and failures are judged. Thus there is good reason to rethink our notions of adulthood. Maguire et al. (2001: 198) make an uncommon (and therefore all the more pertinent) point: "The idea of a 'refusal of adulthood' potentially carries within it the notion that there is a 'normal' version of adulthood which (some) young people are rejecting. There are significant dangers in this interpretation. First, that those who are 'refusers' are in some ways deviant or 'other' and secondly, that there is a fixity in adult status." These critical remarks are exceptions to the rule. Indeed, the largely uncritical manner in which the prevalent perspective is employed by social scientists means that often it simply mirrors the sentiments expressed in the media by marketing and advertising specialists. It is a relationship worth some consideration.

Adulthood, Common Sense, and Sociology

When Theodor W. Adorno remarked on the interdependence of what he called "prescientific thinking" and sociology, he insisted that the former is to be taken seriously: "Unless prescientific interests or extra-scientific concepts are imported into every scientific sociological investigation, then scientific interests and concepts are entirely lacking as well" (2000: 126). Indeed, as Bauman (1990: 10) notes, there is a "special relationship between sociology and common sense." The discipline relies on common sense knowledge as the starting point to analysis. With the help of disciplinary epistemology, or perhaps simply with trained intuition, sociologists defamiliarize the familiar, taken-for-granted assumptions of everyday life and build "second order typifications" (Schütz 1954), theoretical concepts that stand apart from common sense. They build concepts and theories out of the material they find, observe, and study. However, it is not methodologically desirable to privilege common sense above abstraction: "Some historians and sociologists still believe that they can do without conceptual tools altogether and rely exclusively on what they think is plain common sense. But 'common sense' consists of nothing more or less than the abstract concepts and models wrapped up in conventional ways of saying things; as a result, commonsense commentators simply deprive themselves of any possibility of a critical understanding of their own conceptual tools" (Todorov 2003: 7).

Giddens (1984) attempts to reconcile these perspectives. His "double hermeneutic" aims to address the fact that social scientific interpretations of everyday constructs are reinterpreted and reassimilated into lay knowledge. In so doing,

Giddens more than intimates that the quest for second-order typifications never ends. Applying these understandings to our analysis, the sociological notion of an allegedly prevalent delayed adulthood is the second-order typification of lay knowledge about "young people who refuse to grow up." As a second-order typification it has its conceptual origins in common sense, "that rich yet disorganized, non-systematic, often inarticulate and ineffable knowledge we use to conduct our daily business of life" (Bauman 1990: 8).

While sociology rarely concerns itself with an analysis of adulthood as a social category, adult behavior and adulthood as a life stage are implicit in all sociological analyses. From the minutiae of everyday life to the macro processes of globalization; from ethnomethodology to systems theory; from the sociology of knowledge to critical theory to the cultural turn; the actor—whether conceived as individual, as decentered subject, or as system—is an embodiment of adultness. Even when sociologists are explicitly concerned with childhood, adolescence, youth, or old age, adulthood is always present as a point of reference. The adult represents the actor par excellence as the object of the majority of sociological investigations as if, in Norbert Elias's (1978: 248) words, he or she "was never a child and seemingly came into the world as an adult." Thus, adulthood is both undertheorized as a phase of life and taken for granted as a default category and heuristic concept that grounds all manner of analysis. It is as neglected by sociologists as it is ever-present and central to what they do.

The term "practical consciousness," which Giddens (1984)—borrowing from Marx and modifying Schütz's concept of "the natural attitude"—has used in his theoretical work, is useful in this respect. Practical consciousness refers to that prereflexive, intersubjectively constructed stance toward the world that enables individuals to pursue daily life. It is the unarticulated background knowledge that reduces the complexity of everyday interactions largely through their routinization. Elsewhere Giddens further emphasizes the existential centrality of the practical consciousness as "the cognitive and emotive anchor of the feelings of ontological security characteristic of large segments of human activity in all cultures" (1991: 36). Practical consciousness thus refers to a shared repertoire of meanings that confers a measure of predictability on social life and furnishes actors with a stability of reference. Note that sociologists inhabit a practical consciousness other than that which they share with others in their professional field: they are also lay participants in the everyday interactions of the lifeworld. "However hard they might try, sociologists are bound to remain on both sides of the experience they strive to interpret, inside and outside at the same time" (Bauman 1990: 10). They are both subject to and progenitors of commonsense assumptions and second-order typifications. Because of their vocation and the relationship between sociology and common sense, sociologists cannot strictly separate their professional from their everyday practical consciousness. There is therefore considerable overlap between the natural attitudes required in both terrains.

Sociologists are also adults. They have their own memories of childhood, which, like others, they may nostalgically reconstruct; they have their ideas as to what growing up means to them; and it is their own adulthood they embody in the present as the place from where coming of age—their own as well as others'—can be viewed from some distance. As such, adulthood is perhaps for most of us an unproblematic notion. It is not only central and marginal to the discipline, but it is also central and marginal to all adults: central to who they are, and marginal because it is an unobserved part of their identities. The overlap in sociologists' stance toward adulthood as an experiential fact of life and as a disciplinary given contributes to the paradoxical status of adulthood in sociology. Ultimately, it is this paradoxical quality of adulthood as a social representation, its simultaneous centrality and marginality in everyday life, media discourse, and social scientific perspectives that makes it such a rich area of social inquiry.

2

ADULTHOOD, INDIVIDUALIZATION, AND THE LIFE COURSE

"Life should begin with age and its privileges and accumulations, and end with youth and its capacity to splendidly enjoy such advantages."

Mark Twain, Letter to Edward Dimmitt (1901)

The self-aware and autonomous individual is central to the self-understanding of modern societies. In the European imagination its emergence is commonly traced to the Renaissance, when individual identity is said to replace collective identity as the center of subjectivity.[1] With the development of the "ideal of authenticity" around the eighteenth century the subject becomes the full-fledged individual in the modern sense (Taylor 1991: 28). In opposition to those who see the ability to separate right from wrong as a matter of rational calculation, the self is now linked to the belief that human beings have an inherent sense of morality. Charles Taylor (1991) suggests that this moral moment becomes displaced, and authenticity disengaged from its ethical horizons becomes an end in itself. These developments go hand in hand with an increasing freedom of self-determination in fact and as a promise. The promise of freedom remains only partially redeemed. Envisaged by Kant as "humankind's emergence from self-incurred immaturity," on another level it also delivered its opposite: "Standards started to shift, and then there were many of them. The authority of each one came to be cast in doubt, ridiculed or otherwise sapped by another, finding its own indignance reciprocated. A yawning hollowness now spread where once was a centre that held the world, and all its segments, in place" (Bauman 1995: 146).

This "disenchanted" world, as Weber (1992) called it, signaled the emergence of a new imperative: to wrest meaning from existence without the comfort and hope that the belief in a realm beyond the mundane can bring. At the same time the mental security based on "knowing one's station" was traded in for the uncertainties that comprise the other side of relatively greater autonomy. And this all the more so because the world in which we needed to make our own way increased dramatically in scope. As local ties were loosened and state centralization increased, protection and control functions were taken over by the nation-state as a new identity-conferring entity (Elias 1999). Today, in light of the globalization of social relations this abstract scheme of reference has gained in intangibility. Our ethical and moral sense draws on a frame of reference that is unfathomable in its totality, and it is within this context that biographies have become the individual's responsibility to an unprecedented extent. This theme is central to my analysis of contemporary adult lives and bears some further consideration.

Contemporary Individualization

Ulrich Beck's observations of present and emerging forms of sociation are far ranging: changes in the structure of the family and work; the continuing rapprochement of the sexes; the demise of anthropocentrism amid the recognition of ecological risks; and the emergence of issue-based politics and the decline of traditional forms of political affiliation and action. These are all transformations that according to Beck spell the departure of past attitudes, actions, and social life forms. He contends, however, that far from cutting the individual loose from social exigencies, these transformations have chiefly served to reembed subjects in more complex institutional arrangements that demand from them a heightened self-awareness of their biographical trajectories.

The freedom gained by individuals released from traditional social bonds requires that they lead their own lives without the securities of old. While institutional arrangements necessary for society's continuity and reproduction continue to exist, they have to be chosen and prioritized by individuals themselves. This, then, is an "institutionalized individualism" in the manner described by Talcott Parsons with all its ambiguities intact (Beck and Beck-Gernsheim 2002: 163). Jürgen Habermas (1992: 149) too explains this phenomenon succinctly: "On the one hand the person is supposed to achieve greater freedom of choice and autonomy in proportion to his individuation; on the other hand, this extension of the degree of freedom is described deterministically." Bauman (2001a: 9) gets to the heart of the reigning cultural vision:

> The distinctive feature of the stories told in our times is that they articulate individual lives in a way that excludes or suppresses (prevents from articulation) the

possibility of tracking down the links connecting individual fate to the ways and means by which society as a whole operates; more to the point, it precludes the questioning of such ways and means by relegating them to the unexamined background of individual life pursuits and casting them as 'brute facts' which the story-tellers can neither challenge nor negotiate, whether singly, severally or collectively.

Individuals more or less voluntarily carry the burden of responsibility should their attempts at biographical self-determination meet with misfortune. The diminishing reliance on collectively negotiated conditions of life means that unanticipated consequences are attributed to individuals, and are usually perceived by them as personal failures whether or not these are in fact due to systemic factors. It is amid the hegemony of sequestered lives that individualization, far from being descriptive only of emancipatory potentials, also describes an attributive process that renders people increasingly self-accountable: "Social problems can be directly turned into psychological dispositions: into guilt feelings, anxieties, conflicts and neuroses. Paradoxically enough, a new immediacy develops in the relationship between the individual and society: an immediacy of disorder such that social crises appear as individual [crises] and are no longer—or only very indirectly—perceived in their social dimension (Beck and Beck-Gernsheim 2002: 24)."

This process becomes pathological, in the literal sense, when the consequences of decisions are "socially individualized," that is, when their individual shouldering is systemically endorsed. For Honneth (2002b: 146), for example, individualization in its current form signals that "the claims for individual self-realization ... have become institutionalized patterns of expectations and social reproduction to such an extent that their inner purpose has been lost and has, rather, become the foundation for the legitimation of the system." He further argues that in the course of recent history there has been a transformation of "ideals into constraints, of claims into demands" that also gives rise to new forms of social suffering (Honneth 2002b: 155). Not only can the imperative to choose the right course of action and to be self-responsible for one's destiny lead to feelings of alienation and atomization, but contemporary preoccupations with self-realization, the imperative to "be yourself" in addition to structural pressures toward self-responsibility, may well be a key factor in the increasing incidence of depression.[2] In a like manner, Kevin McDonald (1999: 208) suggests that the emergent model of subjectivity, which elevates self-monitoring and strategic action to normative status, gives rise to "new pathologies of the self" afflicting "those who fail to become 'entrepreneurs of the self.'"

Individualization in its current form harbors new dependencies and thus calls for alignments of individual destinies with various institutional demands. Moreover, the individualization of institutional connections, and thus the real and perceived primacy of agency, renders these structural demands obscure; they are consigned to Bauman's "unexamined background" of individual pursuits. But the very fact of individuals' readiness to internalize responsibility and blame, and to take on board not just the positive but, more significantly, the negative consequences of their choices and decisions, presupposes an estimation of self as unique and authentic. The resulting disembeddedness, rather than creating realms of freedom for self-cultivation, creates an increased vulnerability to those forces that play a vital part in shaping the directions of individuals' lives.

Michel Foucault squarely names the ideology under which individualization accelerates: neoliberalism. For Foucault, government includes both the sense of "governing others" as well as "governing the self," and with his concept of "governmentality" he seeks to establish the interpenetration of systemic power relations and subjective self-regulation. In his rendering of Foucault's lecture on neoliberal governmentality, Lemke (2001: 201) unwittingly gives political-ideological context to Beck's nonpartisan circumscriptions:

> The strategy of rendering individual subjects 'responsible' . . . entails shifting the responsibility of social risks such as illness, unemployment, poverty, etc., and for life in society into the domain for which the individual is responsible and transforming it into a problem of 'self-care.' The key feature of the neo-liberal rationality is the congruence it endeavours to achieve between a responsible and moral individual and an economic-rational actor. It aspires to construct prudent subjects whose moral quality is based on the fact that they rationally assess the costs and benefits of a certain act as opposed to other alternative acts. As the choice of options for action is, or so the neo-liberal notion of rationality would have it, the expression of free will on the basis of a self-determined decision, the consequences of the action are borne by the subject alone, who is also solely responsible for them. This strategy can be deployed in all sorts of areas and leads to areas of social responsibility becoming a matter of personal provisions.

Individualization is thus not simply a historical process devoid of power play. Rather, freedom and control are two sides of the same coin. Control, though, is more effective if beliefs give credence to freedom while discrediting notions of control and limitation. The proliferation of options in all spheres of life is a case in point.

Options and Futures

The generation following the baby boomers has been dubbed "the options generation" (Mackay 1997). In fact, it is a commonplace to perceive successive generations as inhabiting a world of increased possibilities and opportunities. The new adults of today are implicated in this proliferation of options, and so it is worthwhile to address this phenomenon. I do so with a truistic, yet often forgotten caveat in mind: modern individuals are not only relatively more able to choose, but to an increasing extent they must do so regardless of whether this is actually possible or not (Beck 1992; Elias 1999: 167; Beck and Beck-Gernsheim 2002). Moreover, they are faced with the task of making choices under conditions of indeterminacy. Bauman (1995: 145) places the imperative to choose at the center of contemporary existential apprehensions: "The anxiety would be lessened, tensions allayed, the total situation made more comfortable, were the stunning profusion of possibilities somewhat reduced; were the world a bit more regular, its occurrences more repetitive, its parts better marked and separated; in other words—were the events of the world more predictable, and the utility or useless-ness of things more immediately evident." Released from the relative certainties of a bygone era (including, for some, the certainty of poverty, sickness, untimely death, and social immobility), the freedom from ascription and a physically pre-carious existence becomes the precarious freedom to choose. Freedom of choice also means that our "search for a centre that holds" (Bauman 1995) is made dif-ficult indeed by an overabundance of alternatives; and it is compounded by an ex-pansion of those domains of life that are perceived as subject to creative agency.[3]

In the present context it is the *perception* of options concerning individuals' biographies that is of greatest interest; and it is not confined to consumption and lifestyle choices, but refers to an orientation toward life per se.[4] With this in mind I suggest that there is a significant affinity between the perception of un-limited options and the promise of eternal life. This affinity is significant insofar as it goes some way toward situating contemporary individuals' attitudes con-cerning the future. Modern individuals are firmly tied to the mundane world of the here and now. Indeed, the good life comes to be perceived as the last and only chance; it is a life that has to be filled with as many experiences as pos-sible, for mortality takes on a new significance with the knowledge that eternity in a *transcendental* mode is clearly no longer an unquestioned fact—the finality of death is now absolute (Rosa 1999). But the transitoriness of life brings in its wake a new validation of life itself, as "the stretch of time between birth and death is our only chance of transcendence, of getting a foothold in eternity . . . We need knowledge [therefore] as to how to reforge transience into durabil-ity: how to build a bridge between finitude and infinity." Indeed, such is "the cunning of culture" that it "allows pillars to be erected on the most friable of foundations which are resilient enough . . . to allow a sense of extemporality to flow into the all-too-temporary life" (Bauman 2001a: 238–39). And it is here, I suggest, that the perception of a profusion of options in all areas of life provides a basis for existential reassurance that is premised on three moments of the contemporary imaginary. First, because the realization of choices is understood to depend on individual commitment (on *my* decisions and no one else's), they appear in principle unlimited. Second, as a consequence no choice has to be ultimate; all choices are theoretically revocable. Third, the very profusion of options, bolstered by the needs structures of capitalist society, renders modern individuals perpetually dissatisfied with the choices made. In full knowledge that other alternatives might just be a step closer to "the real thing"—that there are "unlimited possibilities beyond our reach in fact but not in imagination" (Heller 1985: 304)—our heightened self-awareness has come at the price of the curtailment of our capacity to die "lebensgesättigt," satiated with life (Weber 1992: 88). Life takes on the semblance of an unending selection and decision-making process whose temporal precondition is an open future. As Christopher Lasch (1984: 38) put it, "'freedom of choice' means 'keeping your options open'"—and open choices, I add, call for open time horizons.

The belief in eternity as a collective given is replaced by a secular ersatz eschatology. This "immanentization of transcendence," to borrow from Luhmann (2001: 19), arises from a fundamental psychological need: a sense of control over the future that is particularly prevalent at a time when structural securities are in decline (Mirowsky and Ross 2003: 253–77). To elaborate: however open the future and however unsettling the profusion of options may be, the mere perception of possibilities promises opportunities for decision making and thus agency and control—should one decide to act and make choices and decisions, that is. Moreover, under conditions of individualization that control is systemically cast as subject to individual action. Our "search for a centre that holds" takes place not only in a thoroughly contingent world, but in light of a *potentially controllable* eternity. Therefore, the perception of numerous biographical options, though it burdens us with choice, may provide some relief from what Durkheim saw as the heart of modern anomie—"le mal de l'infini."[5] According to Durkheim, humans have an innate longing for infinity. "[H]uman activity," he says, "naturally aspires beyond assignable limits and sets itself unattainable goals" (1979: 247–48). For Durkheim it is only when unbounded desire is constrained and given shape by society (laws, norms, values, expectations) that there is some hope of contentment.

Now, if the unbounded infinite leads to anomie, then logically the contemporary proliferation and indeterminacy of options would worsen anomic conditions. Indeed, this type of thinking informs much of social theorizing and commentary concerned with an alleged decline of sociability in contemporary culture. Most people, however, cope; and they cope because individualization has delivered to them the mindset that allows them to face the proliferation of options with a degree of confidence: the authentic self, if "actualized," is seen as the means with which to face contemporary uncertainties.[6] This may well be the ideational basis for sentiments such as, "[the future is] contingent, pregnant with potential," expressed by one of my interviewees. I suggest the *belief* that one's personal resources can be marshaled to make the right decision at the right time assuages, for some, the translation of anomic conditions into lived experience. Just as it is immaterial to the believer whether or not God's existence can be proven, so the belief in personal capacities that are subject to individual on demand activation renders secondary concerns whether or not possibilities actually exist. Individuals, in a sense, turn *le mal de l'infini* against itself. In the face of boundless options they nurse a fatalistic faith in their own boundless agency, a "new fatalism" as I call it (see chapter 6). The real and imagined proliferation of options is a double-edged sword. On the one hand, the reduction of possibilities would assuage one of modernity's central anxieties; on the other, in the absence of an unquestionable "collective consciousness" (Durkheim 1960), this would be tantamount to the repudiation of the last chance for transcendence, however mundane its contemporary manifestations. Attitudes that are both held by and attributed to many contemporary young adults—the belief or perception that in principle everything is possible if individual capacities are mobilized; that the future is open-ended; that commitments are until further notice—can be seen as answers to present-day uncertainties that permeate the life course and the individual biography.

Life Course and Biography

There is an image of life that is not easily dislodged from its cultural base: childhood precedes adolescence, which precedes adulthood, which leads eventually into old age, which in turn returns us to childlike dependence. None expressed this image of the life cycle more eloquently than Shakespeare (1971: *As You Like It*, 2.6.139–66), whose work is key in the formation of social representations in Western cultures:

> All the world's a stage,
> And all the men and women merely players:
> They have their exits and their entrances;
> And one man in his time plays many parts,
> His acts being seven ages. At first the infant,
> Mewling and puking in the nurse's arms.
> And then the whining school-boy, with his satchel
> And shining morning face, creeping like snail
> Unwillingly to school. And then the lover,
> Sighing like furnace, with a woful ballad
> Made to his mistress' eyebrow. Then a soldier,
> Full of strange oaths and bearded like the pard,
> Jealous in honour, sudden and quick in quarrel,
> Seeking the bubble reputation
> Even in the cannon's mouth. And then the justice,
> In fair round belly with good capon lin'd,
> With eyes severe and beard of formal cut,

Full of wise saws and modern instances;
And so he plays his part. The sixth age shifts
Into the lean and slipper'd pantaloon,
With spectacles on nose and pouch on side,
His youthful hose, well sav'd, a world too wide
For his shrunk shank; and his big manly voice,
Turning again toward childish treble, pipes
And whistles in his sound. Last scene of all,
That ends this strange eventful history,
Is second childishness and mere oblivion,
Sans teeth, sans eyes, sans taste, sans everything.

This is an image that is close to the bone, because our bodies and minds inexorably grow toward decay. Gene technology has not yet advanced far enough to be able to grant us eternal youth—the realization of a culture's dream. But something is shifting in social reality. The boundaries between childhood and adulthood are blurring, both biologically and socially speaking. Not only are we living longer and often healthier lives than in previous history, our bodies reach sexual maturity at ever-younger ages. While in nineteenth-century Northern Europe the average age of menarche was about 16.5 years, by the last third of the twentieth century the onset of menstruation was around 13 years of age. Male development is also accelerating. While Josef Haydn's (1732–1809) voice broke at 18 and thus he left the boys' choir, Anton Bruckner (1824–1896) did so at 15. Today age 12 or 13 is a common time for boys to resign (Mitterauer 1992: 3–4). The boundaries are also blurring because some contemporary social practices no longer sit comfortably with our ingrained categories of human development and the behaviors and attitudes with which they were—and sometimes still are—associated. The remainder of the chapter attends to this phenomenon and takes into account the interactions between structural constraints, institutional norms, and subjective meaning. For reasons of analytical clarity, I differentiate between life course and biography by distinguishing the institutional standardization of life trajectories from its subjective biographical creation. At the same time, the actual inextricability of life course and biography, of "social structures and human lives," in everyday life is presumed self-evident, even a "sociological truism" (B. Hess 1988: 17).

In *The Rules of Sociological Method* Durkheim states famously that we "may term an institution all the beliefs and all modes of behaviour instituted by the collectivity" (1966: lvi). A few pages further on he asserts: "A social fact is any way of acting . . . capable of exerting over the individual an external constraint; or: which is general over the whole of a given society, whilst having an existence of its own, independent of its individual manifestations" (1966: 13). Researchers often attend to the life course with Durkheim's concepts in mind. Sometimes this is explicitly acknowledged (e.g., Kohli 1986); more often it is implicit in work that posits lives as "culturally and institutionally framed from birth to death" (Heinz and Krüger

2001: 33). Notably, sociologists are mostly concerned to emphasize the enabling facets of the life course, an aspect of external constraint that is perhaps not immediately discernable in Durkheim's writing.[7]

Institutionalized life course is the term used here to denote "a formal set of rules which organize the individual's lifetime progression within social space" (Buchmann 1989: 15). It involves the segmentation of the life course into discrete units by means of codified, formal age norms. In Weber's sense we can speak here of the rationalization of the human life span. Age as an organizational criterion allows the regulation and structuring of life via its "temporalization" (Kohli 1986; Buchmann 1989; Settersten and Mayer 1997). Age codification of life enables governments and bureaucratic institutions to regulate rights and obligations and facilitates the monitoring of compliance through age-structured legislation (e.g., age of consent, child labor, alcohol and tobacco consumption, conscription, the allocation of social provisions and citizen participation rights, and so forth). It also facilitates the definition of individuals' legitimate entry to education, employment, and retirement, allowing the allocation of sequential status positions and roles that link educational achievements to occupational career tracks. This institutionalization along formal rational lines is, for Kohli, the functional equivalent of earlier forms of social control, and is vital to social integration:

> The emancipation of individuals in the transition to modernity did not mean a dissolution of the social structure, but its transformation. Although the biographical room for action and demands for decision-making increased, at the same time a program came into being that constituted, and made predictable, an overall structure to life. No longer was social order reliant on stable conditions of life, but on a regular life course that could be dependably anticipated. The life course . . . constituted a new program for sociation that posited the individual as independently constituted social unit. (Kohli 1990: 25)

The degree of integration is seen to depend on the extent of alignment between individual expectations and aspirations and the template of the life course. Here the state mitigates the complexities and risks arising from individuals' engagement with institutions. It does so by providing age-structured education and employment opportunities as well as social welfare (although there are considerable international differences based on political philosophical traditions concerning the role of the state). While setting limits to individuals' biographies, the life course also provides a frame of reference for the projection of biographies into the future and is as such pivotal to the temporal continuity constitutive of identities.

Life Course and Identity

The life course as a social fact in its modern, rationalized form constrains subjective biographical trajectories. Whether these limits restrict or enable biographical autonomy is a matter of perspective. Kohli, for instance, stresses that a strongly institutionalized life course makes "long-term *biographical perspectives*" and calculable predictability possible (Kohli 1986: 275, original emphasis). Others add that a highly institutionalized life course also allows for the long-term projection of aspirations, because what is attainable and what is out of reach is more or less explicitly structured (e.g., Buchmann 1989: 40–41). Berger and his collaborators (1973) analyzed this situation from a phenomenological point of view, with specific emphasis on the relationship between long-range life planning and identity.[8] They suggest that individuals' common sense background knowledge of social life incorporates an awareness of typically available life. This social matrix for self-projection is vital to individuals' integration through what the authors—borrowing from Robert K. Merton—refer to as "anticipatory socialization." Indeed, they suggest this to be a "basic organizing principle" of society (Berger et al. 1973: 67–72). The assertion that biographical meaning giving must be related to overarching meanings of society clearly resonates with those contemporary theorists who stress that the fit between institutionally furnished opportunities and individual expectations is critical to social integration (e.g., Kohli 1986, 1990; Mayer and Müller 1986; Buchmann 1989; Schwinn 2001). In this view, self-identification relies to a significant degree on individuals' projections of their biographical narrative into the future, which, more than the past, is drawn upon to make sense of everyday life in the present. This not only calls for an alignment of life course and biography, but also depends on the synchronization of individual life trajectories with others' life paths, that is, the establishment of what Glen Elder (1985; 1994) calls "linked lives." The task of guessing one's projected biography and then aligning this precarious design with others' conjectured futures is made possible by "recipe knowledge" (Schütz 1970) of the life course structures within which biographical opportunities are situated.

The Standard Biography

Ideal-typically, the highly institutionalized life course frames the concept of the standard biography. It casts the assumed relative predictability of a life as a function of the alignment between real possibilities and individual aspirations, thereby implying that individual life trajectories have internal continuity as well as social synchronicity with those of similar social positions (i.e., in terms of gender, age, class, and ethnicity). This continuity is most explicitly represented by the sequence of childhood–adulthood–old age that is deeply entrenched in the social imagination as the unfolding of life per se and conforms to our conceptualization of the biological process of growth and deterioration (see Table 1). It is epitomized in the institution of what has variously been called the normal, standard, or tripartite biography (e.g., Kohli 1986; Beck 1992):

Table 1. The Standard Biography in the Social Imagination

	Childhood	Adulthood	Old Age
Private sphere	Family of origin	Family of procreation	"Empty nest"
Public sphere	Education	Work	Retirement
Relationships	Dependence	Independence	Dependence
Competency	Immaturity	Maturity	Decline

Work is central in this schema. Just as work emerges as the taken-for-granted sphere of action around which a human life revolves, so adulthood appears as that (working) stage of life for which childhood prepares, and from which old age departs. The vision of the standard biography is one of a march through the institutions of education, work, and retirement, complemented by equally standardized familial arrangements. The biological schema is reproduced as children leave behind an "empty nest," and enter adulthood themselves. Dependence on school and family is supplanted by the relative independence that an income and living arrangements of one's own afford the adult. Individuals' relationships to significant others and state institutions change accordingly. As old age progresses, social stigmatization often renders the very old infantilized and immature, regardless of actual competencies and abilities (Hockey and James 1993). In keeping with the once-prevalent model of the life cycle, old age returns individuals to the dependencies of childhood.[9]

Particularly during the relatively affluent era following the Second World War, this confluence of life course and biography represented a normative unfolding of life. The emphasis on fulltime employment coupled with comparatively strong welfare-state regulation, under the aegis of a prevalent Keynesian economic policy paradigm, meant that a convergence of objective possibilities and subjective trajectories could indeed occur. And so the standard biography form was rendered a historically specific ideal-typical arrangement of life. As an ideal standard, this model necessarily generalizes and posits life trajectories of some individuals as universally valid. It reflects the lives of individuals for whom access to social and labor market provisions is unhindered by gender, cultural background, and disabilities. In fact, the standard biography is standard insofar as it relies on a taken-for-granted gendered division of labor as the basis for social reproduction and integration (Sørensen 1990; Du Bois-Reymond 1998; Krüger and Baldus 1999). The nuclear, single-income family reliant on a male breadwinner for economic sustenance and a female caregiver responsible for all exigencies internal to the private sphere is, according to this schema, the ultimate reproductive unit. Indeed, the standard biography still prevails as an ideal model with standard adulthood as its center, even though both the actual translatability into experience and individuals' desires to do so have undergone radical changes since the model's zenith in the post–World War II decades.

Devolving Life Course, Fragmented Biographies

Let me highlight some of the more explicit, most general social transformations that render new adults' social environment often radically different from that of their parents' generation. Particular emphasis is placed on Australia, although the trends generally apply to OECD developments.

Education and Work

In the standard biography, education and work are separate and sequential. In social reality, however, education is no longer confined to the first part of the tripartite biography. Rather than ending with entry into the labor market, learning is now a lifelong endeavor. In countries such as Australia, the reduction of government benefits for tertiary students since the early 1980s has meant that most young people enter the workforce before the end of their education. No longer sheltered from the realities of working life, Australian students are more than keenly aware of what "the real world" holds for them long before they are supposed to become part of it in terms of the traditional education-to-work pathway (Dwyer and Wyn 2001). At work, rapid advances in information and communications technology are understood to call for an ongoing updating of knowledge. Here, "the knowledge society" has become a catch-cry for policy initiatives. Learning is seen as the key to security in an insecure work environment, notwithstanding the gap between the vocational promises of education and real employment opportunities. Systemic change allowing for structural transformations is slow at best: "Thus the design of education systems in most parts of the industrialized world still reflects the thinking about the relationship between education and society that was current in the immediate post-war era. School is still seen as the prior educational setting where 'learning' occurs and work is the subsequent setting, where learning is 'applied' . . . [But] the lessons that young people learn are that there are few 'careers,' most work is short-term, and much of it is unskilled. To be successful in employment, people must be flexible and proactive" (Dwyer and Wyn 2001: 25).

As others have also shown and commented upon, for an increasing number of individuals continuous long-term employment in one organization—and even in one career—can no longer be expected (Sennett 1998; Beck 2000; Bauman 2001a). While for Australian baby boomers the median age of entry into the fulltime labor market was around 21, by the year 2000 young people did so around age 27 (Pusey 2003: 80). Young people tend to stay in education for longer and work in temporary jobs before entering the fulltime labor market, or remain in part-time employment beyond the end of their studies (Dwyer and Wyn 2001). Here, as in other countries, a steady deregulation of work has led to its "flexibilization" (ACIRRT 1999) and, like elsewhere, translates into the almost complete liberation of the historically most malleable and today perhaps most acquiescent variable—labor (Gouliquer 2000).[10] Consequently, temporary employment in Australia is among the highest in the OECD at around one-third of the total workforce. These forms of employment with little or no regulated securities are growing fastest (Campbell and Burgess 2001). Indeed, in the nine years from 1990 to 1999 alone temporary employment—or casual employment, as it is termed in Australia—accounted for 71.4 percent of net employment growth (Campbell and Burgess 2001: 175). Other figures show that the measure of casualization has increased by 35 percent in the period 1990–2001 with fulltime employment falling by 8 percent, while the number of people working 49 hours or more has increased by 24 percent from 1990 to 2002 (ACIRRT and CEDA 2002). In addition, among eighteen OECD nations Australia boasts one of the weakest unfair dismissal legislations, indicating that temporal job insecurity has for some time been underwritten by stark bargaining power asymmetries between employers and employees (Tiffen and Gittins 2004: 80–81). The unstable conditions of work caused by the corporate ideal of workforce flexibility mean that working people, and particularly the growing number of temporary employees, must themselves be flexible and ever amenable to change.[11] Significantly, this imperative undermines many young people's plans for the immediate as well as the distant future (Wyn and White 2000; Macdonald and Holm 2002).

Family and Household Formation

There is a trend for (heterosexual) family and household formation to occur later in people's lives. Between 1980 and 1999 the mean age at first marriage has risen from 24 to 28 for women and from 26 to 30 for men, while the number of divorces per hundred marriages has increased steadily from 16 to 41 in the thirty years from 1970 to 2000 across the OECD (Tiffen and Gittins 2004: 190–91). At the same time, blended families and families with same-sex parents are alternative and increasingly socially accepted structural forms alongside the nuclear family norm.

Further, for the fourth consecutive year, in 2004 Australian women in the 30–34 age group had the highest level of fertility (ABS 2004b), while the average age at first childbirth was 27.6 years. This means that 25 percent of Australian women are 35 or older when they have their first child (De Vaus 2005). Moreover, permanent childlessness for women is on the increase. The Australian Bureau of Statistics estimates that 24 percent of women who at present are in their reproductive years will never have children, while recent estimates of permanent childlessness for women in the United Kingdom (20 percent) and the United States (22 percent) show similar trends (ABS 2000).

Living Arrangements

Household constitution is also undergoing significant changes. Partly as a function of the demise of the youth labor market and a prolonged period of education (Wyn and White 2000; Dwyer and Wyn 2001), there is a tendency for young people to remain in the parental home for extended periods or to move back home after some time away (Kilmartin 2000). In Australia, for example, the percentage of people between the ages of 25 and 34 who are cohabiting with their parents has increased from 12.5 percent in 1979 to 24.4 percent in 2000, with the number significantly greater for men (ABS 2000). Statistics Canada data show similar trends. While 27 percent of all those aged between 20 and 29 were living with their parents in 1981, at 41 percent the number had nearly doubled by 2001 (Statistics Canada 2001). Figures in the U.S., on the other hand, are relatively stable. Seven percent of women and 13.5 percent of men between the ages of 25 and 34 were living with their parents in 2003 compared to 7.4 and 10.9 percent respectively in 1960 (USCB 2004b).

Significantly, there is a historically unprecedented trend for young people to move in and out of the parental home several times before settling in their own permanent abode. For example, in the U.K. the proportion of individuals in their twenties who return home after having initially left their parents rose from 25 percent in the late 1950s to 46 percent by 2001 (BBC News 2001). Some of this can be explained by taking into account the erosion of long-term job security as young people are inclined to return to their home base between jobs. In the Australian context, rising house and real estate prices need to be included as significant factors. Interest rates and household debt make home ownership an increasingly unrealistic aim for young people. Following the deregulation of the housing loan sector, "mortgage payments for the average home absorb about twice as much gross disposable family income as a generation ago; as much as three times since 1950 in Sydney," while "overall household and personal borrowing has doubled since 1995" (Pusey 2003: 81). Australia is one of five OECD countries in which housing costs outstripped the overall cost of living between 1995 and 2000 (Tiffen and Gittins 2004: 208–09). Considering the evidence, there are more than enough clues that young people's propensities for episodic returns to or relatively long stays in the parental home are not simply a matter of proclivities on a generational level toward the eschewal of independence. There are, clearly, uncertainties on the structural level that preclude the mapping of medium to long-term life trajectories that feed directly into these trends.

Intimate Relationships and Marriage

The statistics are unambiguous: in Western societies people tend to get married later today than in previous decades. For example, the median age for Australian women at first marriage has risen from 21 to 26 between 1974 and 1998; for men, from 23.5 to 28 years (Carmichael 2002). And while the median age of first marriage for U.S. women was just 20.1 in 1956, it had risen to 25.3 by 2003. In the same time period the mean age for men has increased from about 22 to 27 years (USCB 2004c). These changes are underpinned by large-scale shifts in attitudes and values. In tandem with the "ideal of authenticity" (Taylor 1991), the contemporary era has seen a "transformation of intimacy" whereby intimate relationships tend to be seen as a means toward self-realization and contain an unspoken proviso that liaisons continue "until further notice" (Giddens 1992). At the same time, more than before in Western history, relationships are based on the belief in ideals of intimate mutuality, openness, and equality. Yet, in the absence of socially sanctioned norms of conduct, these relationships balance precariously on the psychological attributes of individuals and their capacity to negotiate their interactions. Thus, people might terminate relationships on relatively intangible grounds, such as the relationship's perceived failure, or its irrelevance to personal objectives, psychological or otherwise. For Bauman (2003), this underwrites the emergence of "liquid love," of intimate bonds that are marked by an utter fragility. However, to link the contingent nature of intimate relationships with an end to commitment per se would be to draw a long bow. While marriage is indeed deferred in Western societies, this says very little about people's willingness to commit to cohabiting. Data giving a more nuanced breakdown (i.e., according to age, socioeconomic position, ethnicity) is difficult to gather. However, we do know that in Australia, for instance, overall heterosexual cohabitation has increased from 1 percent of all couples in 1971, to 10 percent in 1996. We also know that while the divorce rate has risen steadily across the OECD, the rate of remarriage is also relatively high (Tiffen and Gittins 2004: 190–91). What has most certainly changed is the degree of normative validity of heterosexual marriages specifically concerning adult status, because today other forms of relationships compete with marriage as socially validated forms of institutionalized intimacy.[12] Not only are so-called "de facto marriages" (long-term cohabitation of unmarried intimates) common throughout the world, they are often also recognized legally on a par with marriage (e.g., Australia). Similarly, same-sex marriages are steadily on the rise in Western nations. Countries like Canada, Belgium, the Netherlands, South Africa, and Spain recognize gay marriages, for example.

The trade-off for freedom of self-expression and self-development as the requirement for intimate relationships is the uncertainty with which such relationships are beset. Subject not only to career decisions that have to be made by both partners—a historical novelty as a mass social phenomenon—but subject also to contingencies of personal growth, the social and temporal securities that came with unions entered "until death do us part" are no longer the norm. Some twenty-five years ago, in arguably one of the most insightful and prescient pieces of writing on adulthood, Ann Swidler (1980: 127) identified these cultural shifts in the meaning of love and connected the trends to the changing meaning of adulthood: "[T]he emerging love ideology, because it endorses flexibility and eschews permanence, also sees love more as a continuing process than as a once-and-for-all culmination of life, after which people need only live happily ever after. The central elements of the love myth remain; people still seek moral self-definition, fulfilling intimacy, and a meaningful identity. But the framework of expectations about what it means to achieve these things, and thus the cultural definition of adulthood itself, is changing."

Values and Valuations

Most of the changes described above can be traced to structural pressures. However, these have gone hand in glove with cultural changes. As Inglehart (1977) noted, there has been a "silent revolution"—the differential transformation of value orientations across generations that began in the 1950s, gained considerable impetus in the 1960s and 1970s, and continues with the generations' changeover (see also Inglehart 1990; 2003). At this revolution's heart lies a shift from orientations to life that emphasize stability and predictability to points of view that stress subjective values such as personal growth and self-realization. This basic premise has received some support over the last two decades so that we can speak today about a consensus among social researchers and theorists in the area of value research (e.g., Inglehart 1977; 1990; Klages 1993; Wilkinson 1997; Hamilton and Mail 2003), as well as among generalist social theorists and commentators (e.g., Giddens 1991; 1992; Schulze 1992; 2003; Beck 1997; Bauman 2000). Although there are differences, this consensus centers on the diagnosis of increasingly prevalent "postmaterialist" attitudes since the Second World War. An unhappy choice of term, rather than the demise of materialism or consumerism, this refers to the trend to conceive of life per se as subject to individual creativity and the judicious deployment of psychological resources toward the optimization of personal growth and fulfillment.

It is under the aegis of these more recent orientations that shifts in what are considered adult characteristics and priorities are taking place. Thus an Australian longitudinal survey of people born after 1970 ascertained that from a list of eleven "characteristics of adult life," financial independence and making one's own choices and decisions ranked highest, while becoming a parent ranked second last. When asked about "personal priorities," steady work topped the list of fifteen items although this was not connected to a career (ranked 7). And while family and friends were high priorities, marriage and children (ranked 9 and 12 respectively) were not (Dwyer and Wyn 2001: 27). What becomes apparent here is that commitment and stability continue to be important. What is significant is that commitment and stability are weighed up against the maximum achievable level of independence and flexibility.

The Deinstitutionalization of the Life Course

The structural and cultural changes discussed so far are at the core of a devolution of sequential life course programs, or what has been referred to as the deinstitutionalization of the life course (Kohli 1986; 1990). As Buchmann (1989: 186) notes, from the 1970s onward once "highly standardized life trajectories have been 'shattered' by structural and cultural developments in all major social institutions." Rosa, in direct reference to Kohli, perceives these contemporary transformations in terms of a "de-temporalization of life" (2003: 18). The structural shift from an intergenerational to an intragenerational mode is singled out as one example of this transformation. Rosa argues that singular status changes, which once occurred primarily as part of the succession of generations (e.g., one marriage, one family, one job per lifetime), now tend to occur more rapidly, so that it is not unusual for people to marry more often than once, establish more than one family, and frequently change jobs or careers during one lifetime. This denotes a quite radical transformation of the temporal unfolding of the life course with the implication that, while institutional arrangements persist, biographies are no longer beholden to a linear trajectory.

However, there is another dimension to be considered. Institutions themselves often no longer provide temporal securities and thus make the long-term projection of biographies more difficult. This applies to the flexibilization of work as much as to the liberation of marriage from "until death do us part" imperatives. At the same time as this may provide greater biographical flexibility for some, it may well give cause for insecurities for others, especially for individuals who still have the cultural habit of relying on the life course for biographical meaning (Wohlrab-Sahr 1992). Consequently, the standard biography is losing empirical validity for many individuals. Yet, a complete undoing of the tripartite life path is not occurring. After all, children do go to school, and adults for the most part work (or seek work) and later retire. Rather, there is a blurring of the standard life course transitions. In particular, the boundary between adolescence and adulthood is becoming increasingly porous and amenable to individual shifting (Soares 2000). In tacit agreement with Beck's perspective, Wohlrab-Sahr contends that biographies are individualized: "[T]he predictable succession of life stages with their traditional discontinuities and models of coordination of different life spheres is being increasingly replaced and/or overlaid with a series of decisions whose meaning coordinates are subject to individual efforts at connection" (Wohlrab-Sahr 1992: 220).

This challenge to the standard biography may affect the social construction and experience of time since it contains within it the potential to alter individuals' perception of their temporal progress. It may enable or hinder self-identification along a biographical continuum that corresponds with that of others; it may fracture the connections between linked lives, and it may deliver more room for interpersonal negotiation. However, particularly when compared to the immediate postwar era, there is a greater potential for social asynchronicity as individuals are "less likely to experience and/or recognize their own trajectory as part of the 'collective destiny' of the social group(s) to which they belong" (Buchmann 1989: 76). This fragmentation of biographies and their increasing divergence from other biographies is congruent with processes of individualization. Under these conditions the simultaneity of plural, asynchronous, and fragmented biographies becomes a normalized part of the "continuum" of life while, paradoxically, old standards remain ideal evaluative benchmarks.

From Unnecessary Possibility to Impossible Necessity

The very ability to plan for the long term was not only considered a defining characteristic of classic modernity, but was also deemed pivotal to individuals' self-placement in the world, their self-projection into the future, and thus their stable self-identification.[13] By contrast, the contemporary attrition of predictability favors a responsive stance toward life. Since transience and fluidity replace stability and certainty, individuals' "logic of action" is better "oriented toward the present rather than toward the future" (Buchmann 1989: 187). Similarly, Rosa suggests that the loss of structural time perspective engenders a quasi premodern situationalism, whereby self-identification is increasingly taking place against the static background of the present, eschewing the forward motion so indicative of the classic form of modern life. Drawing on Paul Virillio, Rosa (2003: 20) has referred to this phenomenon as the paradox of "accelerated standstill": "The incapacity to engage in long-term commitments and to develop a frame of time-resistant priorities and long-term goals frequently seems to lead to a paradoxical backlash in which the experience of frantic change . . . gives way to the perception of 'frozen time' without (a meaningful) past and future . . . [T]he dynamism of 'classical' modernity, characterized by a strong sense of direction . . . is replaced by a sense of directionless, frantic motion that in fact is a form of inertia."

Such a view contrasts sharply with earlier theorizing about the centrality of long-range life planning to identity formation. Thus, when Berger et al. (1973) wrote their treatise on human consciousness under modern conditions, they did so at a time when long-term, one-track employment and career paths were still the norm. Marriage and family formation, which occurred relatively early in peoples' lives when compared with today, and the long-term perspectives these commitments required and fostered, reciprocated this order. The paradox about the exigency of long-term planning, at a time when for many this was a real possibility, is that under such conditions it was not imperative; the long term was lived experience, and the future could still be envisaged with a fair degree of certainty, in material terms at least. As such, it was perhaps impossible to foresee, conceptualize, and theorize identity formation under different, more tenuous circumstances. By contrast, the unpredictability of the present requires continuous reflection concerning one's biography. This is a salient, and on the individual level perhaps the most immediately applicable, empirical instance of what some social theorists mean when they refer to contemporary modernity's "reflexivity." (e.g., Giddens 1990; Beck et al. 1994). It is also a singular situation; for while there has been a historical shift from the unnecessary possibility to the impossible necessity of life planning, the unpredictability of contemporary life means that this is only effective over the short term. We can now unpack what has been deemed a contemporary "culture of the present" (Mongardini 1996): the imperative to plan comes up against the reality of the only comprehensible time frame in which this is now possible—the here and now and, perhaps, the most immediate future. Bauman's (2001: 231, original emphasis) thoughts resonate with contemporary social conditions and the experiences they frame:

> Identities of postmodern men and women remain, like the identities of their ancestors, human-made. But they no longer need to be meticulously designed, carefully built and rock solid. Their most coveted virtue is *flexibility*: all structures are to be light and mobile so that they can be rearranged at short notice, one-way streets are to be avoided, no commitment should be so strongly binding that it cramps free movement. Solidity is anathema, as is all permanence—now a sign of dangerous maladjustment to the rapidly and unpredictably changing world, to the surprise opportunities it holds and the speed with which it transforms yesterday's assets into today's liabilities.

Hence, the reputed presentism—living in the present for its own sake—which has become a rarely reflected upon trope supposed to describe young adults' attitudes to life is inaccurate. More accurately, "what is lost is not the future, nor is it time, but a unitary social pattern for the formulation of orientations for the future" (Krüger and von Wensierski 1991: 250). Indeed, the differentiation and individualization of horizons of opportunity has structuring effects on young adults' everyday frame of mind. To foreshadow a thematic of chapter 6, they often concentrate on the here and now because planning for the future is simply too difficult. What they can do, however, is dream. They can project their aspirations into an amorphous future and try to hold on to plans which are often multiple and almost always unhinged. There are also marked differences between the generations. Having been born into this world, and having acquired these taken-for-granted aspects of what it means to live with uncertainty is in stark contrast to growing up in Hobsbawm's Golden Age. Settling down is, as we shall see, not only no longer desirable for many young people, but increasingly impossible when the social prerequisites for this to occur are diminishing. What their parents' generation may judge as thoroughly precarious conditions of life are normal to those contemporary young adults who have never known things to be different. This needs to be taken into account when one generation of researchers attends to the practices of another; and when they take the standard adulthood of another time as the yardstick by which they judge present-day practices.

The Choice Biography and Its Limits

As noted earlier, individualization flows from the loosening of explicit structural ties, leading to the transformation of dependent into self-fashioned lives. Social, political, and economic conditions support the cultural ideal of "a life of one's own" (Beck and Beck-Gernsheim 2002). The individual life story is said to have become a "do-it-yourself" or "choice" biography:

> Individualization in this sense means that each person's biography is removed from given determinations and placed in his or her own hands, open and dependent on decisions. The proportion of life opportunities which are fundamentally closed to decision-making is decreasing and the proportion of the biography, which is open and must be constructed personally is increasing. Individualization of life situations and processes thus means that biographies become self-reflexive . . . Decisions on education, profession, job, place of residence, spouse, number of children and so forth, with all the secondary decisions implied, no longer can be, they must be made. (Beck 1992: 135)

This individualization of life trajectories must occur within the limits of existing opportunity structures. To illustrate: while many parents can choose the type of school they want their child to attend, a minimum education is compulsory in Western societies. Further, in countries such as Australia, the U.S., and Britain the choice of school and/or university or college depends on parents' financial wherewithal. The prospective educational institution's proximity to home, public transport infrastructure, and prestige (which may determine further life chances) are other considerations that limit the options. Apart from class, ethnicity, and gender, age too sets limits on the flexibility of individual biographies, that is, on the "proportion of the biography which is open and must be constructed." Consider childhood: children's institutionalization into the life course is from the very beginning undertaken for them, and thus their biographies, even in adolescence, evince less of the do-it-yourself quality said to be indicative of contemporary life trajectories than it would seem at first. The very old, the frail, and the disabled are subject to similar dynamics of dependency.

Restrictions apply to younger adults as well. Although adulthood represents that stage of life that is most readily connected to competencies and opportunities to exercise autonomous choice, these too are in some respects limited. For example, for most people there is little choice in regards to work. The very question whether one actually wants to work is for most decidedly a non-option. Beyond the need to earn enough money to afford a minimum of material comfort and psychological security for oneself and/or one's dependents, work is crucial to the attainment of a level of recognition in exchange for one's contribution, achievement, and success in societies where work is central to social and self esteem (Honneth 1996). Socio-economic background, individuals' abilities and their formal recognition through various professional and educational forms of accreditation, the ebbs and flows of national labor markets, policy decisions as well as global economic conditions, delimit desired biographical designs. In short, we can only engage in work if openings are actually available.[14] Additionally, there are links between the attainment and continuity of work and perceived productive limits of age. There are strong suggestions that the upper limit of what is considered a productive age is receding to an ever-younger glass ceiling.[15] The imperative of choice does not imply the autonomous exercise of choice. Kohli's (1990: 29) remark with reference to the labor market is opposite here: "In so far as the market power of employees continues to exist due to the continuance of institutional security, flexibilization means, in fact, an increase of chances for action. Insofar as they are forced to expose themselves to the vicissitudes of the labor market without such security this rather constitutes a backslide to situational life forms that have little to do with individualization in the sense of possibilities for autonomous choice." A more balanced consideration of choice is clearly necessary in order to differentiate between actual and perceived options. While there may be a belief that as long as we have the required will we can be whoever we want to be, work in whatever field we desire, and partake in particular kinds of relationships, the simple fact is that reality confronts us with restrictions and constraints whose social origins may well be veiled by perceptions and worldviews.

Options Surplus and Foreclosed Futures

The weakening of the temporal reliability of institutions does not undermine notions of temporal continuity as far as ongoing personal development is concerned. Indeed, the perception of a surfeit of options in all spheres of life irrespective of their actual existence or nonexistence offsets the ostensible mismatch between subjective (psychological) development and the experience of structural discontinuity. For one, episodic experiences do not necessarily constitute a hindrance to personal development; they can also be perceived as prerequisites. For example, many young people slot extended periods of travel between education and work in order to accumulate "experiences" (Erlebnisse). Likewise, relationship breakups occur not only because of explicit incompatibilities, but also because experience in the sense of an accumulation of knowledge (Erfahrung) is sometimes considered good preparation for the "real thing." Thus, the openness of the future—perceived as such because of the temporal unreliability of structural conditions and a sense of abundance of options—helps to legitimate the postponement of ultimate choices. There is, then, an affinity between the perception of life as an unlimited process of development and the proliferation of options, a theme that is further developed in chapter 6. For now it suffices to note that the contingencies arising from the transformation of the life course and its biographical navigations affect the transitions to and ultimately alter the meaning of adulthood.

The Individualization of Transitions

The economic and social changes of the recent past have meant that the markers indicating a transition from adolescence to adulthood either are absent or have become individualized and have thus lost the social significance they once held. Markers of transition are individually identified as such rather than socially prescribed. When people are asked to identify such markers, they may mention various heterogeneous events or moments: getting your driver's license, any number of "firsts," helping a family member conquer trauma, and so forth (see chapter 5). Transitions such as these are no longer comparable with collectively understood rites of passage—rituals at the end of which lies adulthood. They are individual experiences that are often retrospectively assigned symbolic transitionary meaning by the individuals themselves in an ad hoc fashion. As such, these transitions no longer constitute social markers of adulthood in the strict sense (Arnett and Taber 1994; Arnett 1997; 2004).

Yet, however characteristic this individual sense-making may be of modernity's individualizing tendencies, it neither indicates a total separation from collective identifications, nor does it lend credence to the notion of an exclusively psychological adulthood (Côté 2000: 19). We know at least since Maurice Halbwachs (1992) that individual memories themselves are socially derived. By definition, this means that even those markers of transition that are individually chosen to represent rites of passage, however ad hoc, and however much they appear to signify atomized individuals, are obtained from preexisting typifications. To illustrate: though possible, it is highly unlikely that someone would pick their first game of badminton, going to the movies, or plucking their eyebrows as markers of transition to adulthood. It is undoubtedly more likely that someone would choose to assign their first sexual experience, their first independent purchase, or giving birth some transitionary significance. This is so because—however hidden, tacit, or implied; however unconsidered or even denied—there is a collectively constituted, shared, and more or less decipherable universe of meaning in which we realize our individual continuity: culture, society, present as well as past. Arnett's thesis that markers of transition are becoming individualized therefore needs qualification: no matter to what extent events and experiences are subject to individual sense-making, the range of choices is still culturally delimited, the patterns open to imitation. However innovative we are as creative beings, "innovation is not entirely arbitrary: the possible histories are pregiven. Without 'history' a subject cannot establish her homeostasis and fashion her own history from the past" (Henning quoted in Schroer 2000: 445).

At the same time, the devolution of the classic markers and the predominance of personally significant events is in line with the view that the boundaries between adulthood and (depending on the authors) childhood, adolescence, or youth are blurring (Lenzen 1991; Furlong and Cartmel 1997; Soares 2000; Lee 2001). Support for this perspective is drawn variously from contemporary social contingencies and the practices and orientations with which they are negotiated. Undeniably, it makes little sense in today's world for young people to strive for a career modeled on those that were tenable in previous decades, and neither might they want to. They may just as well find themselves back in the education system after some time out, traveling, or working part-time. Just as work continuity is becoming passé, so marriage is delayed and sometimes constitutes merely one among a range of lifestyle options, while having children is now more likely to become a reality in people's thirties rather than twenties, if at all. These are the social phenomena that constitute the bases for the delayed adulthood thesis and its ideal-type, standard adulthood—a standard of judgment that is no longer adequate to the present. Reconsiderations are due. In the remaining chapters I will elaborate an alternative viewpoint.

3

ADULTHOOD AND SOCIAL RECOGNITION

"I am genuinely free only when the other is also free, and recognized as such by me. This freedom of the one in the other unites human beings in an internal way, whereas in contrast, need and necessity bring them together only externally and contingently."

G. W. F. Hegel, *Philosophy of Subjective Spirit* (1830)

Ambiguities about adulthood call for a fresh perspective, one that accounts for the social realities that underpin its changing meaning on the societal and on the individual level. Because adulthood is in the final analysis a social category, this reconceptualization is arguably best undertaken by stressing the intersubjective nature of the constitution of meaning in society no matter how pluralized contemporary structures of meaning may be, and how individualized they may appear. The continuity of human sociability—and ultimately human autonomy—continues to depend on the validation of a diverse array of individual practices, perspectives, and mentalities by others. From this standpoint, the open institutional and cultural arrangements of modernity imply an interpretation of society as "institutionalized recognition order" (Honneth 2003: 138). That is to say, beyond the contradictions of class-based interests—the earlier centerpiece of critical theory (Honneth 2002a)—lies the granting and withholding of social recognition as a driver of social change. At first blush, Honneth's conception lends itself most readily to social movements and their collective claims for recognition that, historically speaking, have provided the impetus for social change. It is in this sense that Charles Taylor (1994) has taken up the notion of recognition, for example. In this book, however, I have adapted the concept of recognition toward a better understanding of the social situation of contemporary young adults. As already noted, although the realities of today diverge considerably from those of the past, the social significance of the notion of adulthood has by no means diminished. I suggest that this is so because the social recognition and respect that accompany adult status are central to individuals' self-identification as "full partners in interaction" (Fraser 2000: 113). Thus, to be adult in contemporary society means to be recognized as a full person at different levels of social interaction, ranging from law to the various conventions of different social milieus.

This view needs to be elaborated not least because it is drowned out by another, which sees identity formation—qua individuation—as a struggle between polar opposites: society/collectivities on the one hand, the individual on the other. This view is particularly pertinent in the present context, because it is most closely aligned to everyday notions of self-realization and personal growth, recurrent themes in subsequent chapters. This perspective is also highly commensurate with the ideal of the self-sufficient, self-responsible market actor averse to external constraints and regulation; and it has, in a neat alignment between neoliberalism and pop psychology (its self-referential therapeutic), become the commonsense prescription of subjectivity.

Jung's Vision and Commonsense Identity

The question "who am I?" is as central to contemporary individuals' self-understanding as this question has become increasingly pressing in the course of modernity. For Jung (1977a: 448), individuation "is the process by which individual beings are being formed and differentiated; in particular, it is the development of the psychological individual as a being distinct from the general, collective psychology. Individuation, therefore, is a process of differentiation, having for its goal the development of the individual personality." This differentiation from collective psychology, however, is not analogous with atomization. Rather, it refers to the integration of unconscious and conscious elements of the psyche that are conceived as part of humanity at large: "As the individual is not just a single, separate being, but by his very existence presupposes a collective relationship, it follows that the process of individuation must lead to more intense and broader collective relationships and not to isolation" (Jung 1977a: 448). Yet, society is the antithesis to the individual: "Individuation and collectivity is a pair of opposites, two divergent destinies. They are related to one another by guilt. The individual is obliged by the collective demands to purchase his individuation at the cost of an equivalent work for the benefit of society. . . . What society demands is imitation or conscious identification, a treading of accepted, authorized paths" (Jung 1977b: 452). This imitation of approved social action needs to occur until an "equivalent" beneficial to society has been found and individuals can be "exempted" from mimicking prescribed behaviors (1977b: 452). Just as society is perceived as an entity existing outside the individual, underpinning this conception of psychological development is Jung's positing of an existing true self situated in the unconscious. This self— an anthropological constant—strives toward realization or actualization. As a central part of Jung's vision, the will to self-realization as the driving force of individuation has become widely influential in psychotherapy, so much so that his disciples are moved to propound statements such as, "I believe that any psychotherapy founded on depth psychology should focus above all on the question of who we really are above and beyond the distortions provoked by the way we were brought up or by the society we live in" (Jacoby 1990: 96). This avowal amounts to the hypostatization of the self, an essentially mythical entity in Jung. But although in such contemporary versions Jung's thought is perhaps taken to its extreme conclusions, they nonetheless arise from his oppositional positioning of individual and society. This dichotomy between an essential self waiting to be revealed, realized, and experienced in all its fullness and external demands is a pivotal cultural precept and guiding belief for new adults, as chapter 6 shows. But the question "who am I?" cannot be separated from its qualifier: "who am I in the eyes of others?" Our self-identifications and self-perceptions, our self-placement in our social environment, and in fact our very constitution as social beings hinge on validation by others—by family, friends, and lovers as much as legislatures, bureaucracies, and markets.

Social Recognition: A Selective Overview

From the moment we realize that our infantile omnipotence is no more than a presocial fantasy, and that our autonomy relies on our becoming active collaborators in the mutual constitution of the mother-child bond, we depend on those social dynamics that engender self-confidence, self-respect, and self-esteem, to foreshadow Honneth's typology. In turn, we use our own estimation of others to categorize them in order to anticipate the likely rules of interaction. Some time before social recognition became a discrete research area in sociology, Erving Goffman (1986: 2), analyzing microsocial processes, noted: "When a stranger comes into our presence . . . first appearances are likely to enable us to anticipate his category and his attributes, his 'social identity.' . . . We lean on these anticipations that we have, transforming them into normative expectations, into righteously presented demands." These are the more intimate moments of social interaction. They may be seen as replicating on the micro level those institutionalized and legislated forms of recognition that, for modern individuals, have become the social foundation upon which their self-understanding, and ultimately the self-understanding of their societies, rests. Thus knowing who we are is also inseparable from knowing who we can be, and from having as part of our natural attitude an understanding of the normative possibilities for our flourishing as human beings. This basic precept forms the foundation for the concept of social recognition in sociology.

Although Johann Gottlieb Fichte (1762–1814) was perhaps the first continental philosopher to devote himself to the subject, it is G. W. F. Hegel's (1770–1831) writing on the "struggle for recognition" in his *Grundlinien der Philosophie des Rechts* (Philosophy of Right) (1983 [1819/1820]) that provided the impetus for the concept's entry into sociology.[1] Recognition has in various ways and to various degrees of explicitness entered into interpretations of the relationship between the individual and society in the works of such thinkers as George Herbert Mead, Georg Simmel, Max Weber, Ervin Goffman, and Jürgen Habermas. However, a systematic social-theoretical attempt to outline the shifting dynamics of recognition in modernity was first proposed by Honneth in his *Struggle For Recognition: The Moral Grammar of Social Conflict* (1996), the original version of which was published in Germany in 1992. Taylor (1994) took up this thread in his political philosophy with a particular emphasis on ethnic and national identities in the context of multiculturalism, while Nancy Fraser contributed to a critical understanding of the term from the perspective of moral and political philosophy (1995; 2000; 2001; Fraser and Honneth 2003). Others, such as Avishai Margalit (1996) and Tzvetan Todorov (1996), have further marshaled the concept in political philosophy. My own discussion takes its lead from Honneth's work, and from other sociologists who have based their work on the recognition-theoretical turn in critical theory.

At first glance, present uncertainties about the contemporary biography, and by extension adulthood, would seem to fit concerns of postmodern theorists who, according to Honneth, tend to maintain that subjects' "possibilities for freedom are best realized when, independent of all normative expectations and bonds, they are able to creatively produce self-images" (1995a: 225). Indeed, contemporary individuals, released from the normative constraints of old, appear to have immense freedoms for experimentation with images of the self. After all, notions such as delayed adulthood conjure up not only a reputed deferral of independence, stability, and responsibility, but also the open-endedness and contingencies of a continuing youthful fascination with various lifestyles. However, as Taylor (1991) has pointed out, we need socially validated horizons of significance against which to attempt self-constitution. Honneth is in tacit agreement with Taylor when he responds to the "self-misunderstanding" of social theories that treat processes of deinstitutionalization as facilitative of self-actualization. He reinterprets Hegel's notion of social recognition and pits it against his own reading of postmodern theory: " Thus, on this interpretation, the freedom of self-realization is not measured according to the distance the individual can establish between himself and the cultural lifeworld, but accordingly to the degree of recognition he can find in his social environment for his freely chosen goals: instead of being defined by the scale of distance from all normative bonds, the increase in personal individuality is determined here by the degree to which individual differences are communicatively granted, indeed encouraged" (1995a: 227). In this view, recognition is a fundamental human necessity; its presence or absence (in the form of disrespect or "misrecognition") informs our self-understanding as humans: "People strive for recognition because they need recognition" (Holtgrewe et al. 2000: 11). Hegel's struggle for recognition is fundamentally a struggle that is constitutive of subjects' identity and by definition precludes poststructuralist notions of the "decentred" subject (e.g., Lacan 1968).

George Herbert Mead (1934) elaborated this position from his social-psychological perspective on identity formation and provides one of Honneth's conceptual springboards. Mead's perspective stands in contrast to Jung's idea of individuation that, while acknowledging the importance of society to the development of integral individual selves, posits society as the negative foil against which individuation is to occur. For Mead, on the other hand, society is more than a background of collective representations: his vision is one of mutuality and interpenetration of individual and society. In Mead there is a tension between the socially projected Me and the subjective viewpoint of the I. Individuals internalize the way "significant others" act toward them, and in so doing they take on the expectations of others as normative. Our interpretation of who we are in the eyes of others constitutes Mead's Me, without which neither social action nor individuation is possible. The I, the source of unique, creative impulses, is in constant reflexive tension with the Me. It reacts to the perspectives of significant others and learns that not only conformity, but also acting against the norms of the Me is possible. The successful reconciliation of I and Me results in an integrated self, a self, it must be noted, that is both socially generated and individually developed. But this is not necessarily so. Our "striving for recognition has a double character. When striving for recognition is not linked to an autonomous identity it is the basis of a compulsory orientation to the judgments of others, the foundation of social conformity," akin to what Riesman diagnosed as the "other-directed character" (Holtgrewe et al. 2000: 12). This interaction of social environment and individual self-identification is pivotal to theories of social recognition.

Honneth's Typology

Honneth utilizes both Mead and Hegel as his informants and further develops social recognition with a tripartite typology that forms the cornerstone of his interpretation of "bourgeois-capitalist society as an institutionalized recognition order" in an attempt "to show that the distinctively human dependence on intersubjective recognition is always shaped by the particular manner in which the mutual granting of recognition is institutionalized within a society" (Honneth 2003: 138).

The first kind of social recognition Honneth identifies, "love," refers to a type of affective recognition that is vital to individuals' trust in their physical integrity and the value of their physical and emotional needs. We gain this type of self-confidence, as Honneth calls it, through primary socialization and in intimate relationships where it is ideally reaffirmed by the experience of intimacy, of care. Recognition through love began to be officially institutionalized in systems of education at the time of the emergence of childhood as a discrete stage of life—of the conception of children as beings having unique rights to protection and nurture (Ariès 1973). In a parallel development, the relationship between women and men was freed from economic and other social constraints and came to be anchored in feelings of mutual affection. Intimate relationships underwent a re-interpretation of meaning and became institutionalized as "love-marriage," that is, "as the institutional expression of a special kind of intersubjectivity, whose peculiarity consists in the fact that husband and wife love one another as needy beings" (Honneth 2003: 139). Recognition through mutual affection and care becomes a prerequisite for individuals' self-confidence in their bodily integrity. Second, recognition in the form of "law" refers to the legislation of individual rights and obligations regardless of people's "origin, age or function" (2003: 139). Through the historical change in the recognition order of society from feudal to democratic institutional arrangements, individuals gained what Honneth calls self-respect: a self-understanding as persons with socially acknowledged, validated, and institutionalized rights and duties that, in principle, render individuals equal moral partners in interaction. The third form of recognition, "solidarity," is also related to changes from traditional to modern societies. Feudal-traditional hierarchies, based on social honor determined by birth and social position, were superseded by social esteem based on the recognition of individuals' unique traits and abilities—their "endowments," as Heller (1993) calls them—and the contributions they make in accordance with existing social values and goals. Because the "achievement principle" (Leistungsprinzip) is the central evaluative factor in capitalist societies, Honneth puts a decided emphasis on work. Work constitutes the relevant "intersubjectively shared value-horizon" conducive to the elevation of individual achievement as the prime standard for social esteem, and thus for self-esteem (1996: 121). This is supported by Robert E. Lane, whose study shows unambiguously that "[a] person's . . . self-respect and self-reliance will depend more on the labour market than on the consumer market" (Lane 1991: 24).

Honneth's three forms of recognition bring into relief three parallel forms of disrespect (see especially Honneth 1995b). The obverse of love is a loss of self-confidence in the integrity of and the autonomous control over one's body. This form of disrespect is most explicitly encountered in cases of rape or torture. The flip side of self-respect, Honneth suggests, is marked by its loss through structural exclusion. This withholding of equal legal status causes in individuals the feeling that they are not recognized as full and equal partners in interaction, that they lack the moral competence to fully partake in society. The form of disrespect related to achievement is anchored in the loss of self-esteem through the withholding of recognition for individuals' specific traits, abilities, and contributions. We could think here of the marginalization of people on account of race and ethnicity, the continued nonvaluation of housework, and the social ostracism to which the unemployed are subjected on the grounds of their perceived noncontribution to society. However, because recognition is an equalizing concept, and as such is distinguished from the explicitly hierarchical notions of prestige and honor, inequality has its source not in less recognition, but in the denial of recognition.

There is another, complementary sense in which social recognition can be understood, one that is particularly pertinent in the present context. Voswinkel puts it succinctly when he suggests that recognition "is the medium of social integration that transmutes social norms and values into subjective identities" (Voswinkel 2002: 67). Once again, the mutuality of individual and social processes is emphasized here. Recognition as the medium of integration ensures that individuals assimilate the prevalent cultural norms. In practice, this assimilation is dependent on prevailing relations or dynamics of recognition (Anerkennungs-verhältnisse). This is important to Honneth, who is concerned "to show that the distinctively human dependence on intersubjective recognition is always shaped by the particular manner in which the mutual granting of recognition is institutionalized within a society" (Honneth 2003: 138). However, assimilation is not synonymous with adaptation. Individuals make claims for recognition and thus contribute to changes in the relations of social recognition through their practices—from the actions of everyday life to the collective actions of social movements. Importantly, particularly in times of rapid social transformation, there is always the possibility that some criteria for recognition lag behind social practice, that "the 'old order' can become the yardstick against which new conditions, new promises and their agents are measured" (Holtgrewe et al. 2000: 18). This possibility of rupture between new conditions and old standards represents a conceptual link to the normative lag between standard adulthood and contemporary practices and makes possible its further elaboration.

Adult Recognition and Personhood

To reiterate my discussion thus far: adulthood is central in the social imagination as the long middle of human life. It is the central social stage of the institutionalized life course and the standard biography, both of which are models for conduct that were unchallenged from about the middle of the nineteenth to the last third of the twentieth century. Adulthood is central to sociology, although it constitutes an unarticulated background to most sociological investigations. This very centrality of adulthood goes hand in hand with a particular ideology that is vital not only to the experience of adulthood, but to the experience of childhood and old age as well: the equation of adulthood with full personhood. Eisenstadt (1971: 30) hints at this when he contends, "[t]here is . . . one focal point within the life span of an individual which is to some extent emphasized in most known societies, namely the achievement of full adult status, or full membership in the social system." More recently, Hockey and James (1993) attended to this ideational dominance of adulthood in their investigation of forms of marginalization based on age and ability. According to their analysis, "personhood in Western society is symbolized through the ideas of autonomy, self-determination and choice"—constitutive aspects of what it means to be a full person, a full member of society, that are in their very association with adulthood omitted from conceptions of childhood and old age (Hockey and James 1993: 3). That is to say, our culturally specific framing of childhood and old age depends on the withholding or nonattribution of autonomy, self-determination, and choice from the very young and the very old. So powerful is the association of adulthood with personhood that adults who do not embody ideals of full competence, such as adults with disabilities, the infirm, and the frail are by way of infantilization relegated to the margins, to a quasi-childhood: "Overdependency and non-reciprocity are considered childish traits, and adults who have them—even if it's not their fault—suffer a reduction in status. This is one reason why the severely disabled and the very old are often treated as children" (Murphy quoted in Hockey and James 1993: 72).

When adulthood is seen as the point of reference for the social construction of dependency, the unequal distribution of power according to age biases comes to the fore: "[the] passage through the life course . . . involves the wielding and attribution of personhood at different times and . . . power is asymmetrically wielded as individuals move between marginal and central social positions, between different conceptions of personhood. Parents, for example, are persons in a way which small children are not; adults are persons in ways that 'the elderly' no longer are. And in each relationship, power is unevenly exercised" (Hockey and James 1993: 45). This is not to say, however, that adulthood qua personhood becomes yet another key to unlocking the core of social inequality in modern societies. Rather, it highlights the great complexity of extant power asymmetries, particularly when the notion of personhood is cast against the more established categories of gender, social class, and ethnicity (Hockey and James 1993: 45). Whether it is the infantilization of the old and disabled, the social construction of childhood as a time of vulnerability as well as harboring the vestiges of delinquency, or the infantilization of women ("babes") or nonwhites ("boys"); whether it is the gradual attrition of working-class precociousness and the universalization of middle-class childhood (Gillis 1981; Perrot 1997), adulthood is a metaphor for membership in society through the attainment of full personhood. As a metaphor, it cuts across divisions of gender, sexuality, ethnicity, and class while its experience is, at the same time, contingent on these drivers of social inequality. Adulthood, then, denotes individuals' status in society as full partners in interaction. Personhood as the attainment of autonomy, self-determination, and choice cannot be divorced from relations of "adult recognition," the term used here to emphasize the social acknowledgement of adult status. The centrality of adulthood in modern life "has less to do with its position mid-way through the span of human life than with its apparent *desirability*" (Pilcher 1995: 81, original emphasis) as the achievement of social recognition. Our cultural association of adulthood with personhood is the meaningful constant of this social category even though social actors are continuously redefining its content. Therefore the actual postponement or rejection of adulthood as claimed by proponents of the delayed adulthood thesis would thus entail a deferral or rejection of personhood. I suggest that this is not so. Rather, I propose that what is taking place is a redefinition of the normative ideal of adulthood, of its most entrenched expectations and representations at the level of everyday practices while the equation of adulthood with personhood remains an orientating reference point.

Research including the findings presented in chapters 5 and 6 confirms that for contemporary young adults, personhood is often based on their own evaluation of competencies (e.g., Arnett 1997; Du Bois-Reymond 1998). Yet, this self-understanding is frequently not matched by external validation. Here, social science and media discourse bemoaning the passing of standard adulthood for reasons of an alleged generational immaturity plays a significant role; it amounts to a withholding of recognition on the discursive level. At the same time, new adults tend toward the rejection of those aspects of standard adulthood that connote conventionality, rigidity, and an end to more varied forms of sociability (see chapter 6). Recognition is most readily attainable in the labor market, where flexible selves, that is, individuals who neither expect loyalties from their employers nor evince loyalties to the stabilities of old, are rewarded as ideal employees. The law too recognizes citizens. This tension between self-recognition and the repudiation of conventional adulthood on the one hand and between structural recognition and discursive misrecognition on the other is tantamount to a recognition deficit. This recognition deficit is emphatically not the result of a one-way process; it is intersubjectively constituted.

Adult Recognition and Social Change

The classic markers of adulthood (marriage, parenthood, work, and independent living) can be assigned specific criteria for adult recognition that were particularly entrenched in the immediate postwar decades. While losing empirical salience, they retain their normativity on the ideational level and are as such readily iterated when the meaning of adulthood is articulated (chapter 5). Thus *marriage* attracts adult recognition because it connotes the achievement of adulthood anchored in the social recognition of individuals as *committed* and *responsible*. This form of recognition is highly gendered. Historically, for women marriage meant a shift from one kind of dependence to another: from the family of origin (or families to which women were tied as service personnel) to dependence on their husbands (Sørensen 1990). While this underscores the point that adult independence in the European tradition mainly pertained to men, it must be considered that marriage for women still meant more than a mere continuity of dependence. It entailed a shift in status from daughter/sister to wife/mother that came with the added responsibilities of a household of one's own, even if this meant doing the majority of unpaid housework.

Parenthood means that you are sharing the same burdens and pleasures as so many others. It entails a kind of adult recognition that is reliant upon the existence of at least one other human being (a child) for normative force. This is adulthood as a function of the social recognition of the shared demands, challenges, and joys of parenthood, of one's ability to extend care to others and into the future to another generation. To somewhat liberally appropriate a term coined by Erikson (1950), this is recognition based on *generativity*.

Independence attained through *work* leads to social recognition based on *performance* and *productivity*, on one's contribution to society in societies where work is a central hub on which the validation of personhood hinges (Honneth 1996). Intimately connected to work, *independent living* connotes adulthood as a function of the social recognition of independence gained through the transformation of productive competencies into creative action. This is recognition based on *creativity*, which is perhaps best expressed by the colloquialism "having something to show for."

In sum, adult recognition through commitment and responsibility, productivity and performance, generativity and creativity, implies that being adult is not something we can simply claim for ourselves. Individuals' adult status ultimately relies on the extent to which the things they do and say, and the attitudes and beliefs they hold and express, match the social norms or criteria and expectations of what constitutes adult behavior and attitudes in society in different contexts and at different times. Subjective identifications and social validation intertwine. The more closely our practices and behaviors match the normative expectations of adulthood, the more deeply etched in individuals' self-perception and bearing will be their self-understanding as adults. Again, from this perspective the personalization of adulthood has its limits; it can only to a very narrow degree be subject to individual decision making, whatever personal perceptions.

This typology highlights the kinds of recognition attained once certain objective identifiers of adult status are realized. Particularly as coinciding benchmarks (as a "package deal"), these markers of adulthood can be considered entry points to standard adulthood, a form of adulthood specific to the immediate post–Second World War era, and thus specific to a particular generation. In fact, they were *more* than ideals for the postwar generation; they were achievable milestones for the majority of individuals in Western societies at that time. The relations of adult recognition were institutionalized at various levels of everyday life. Culturally represented in TV shows, radio programs, Hollywood movies, and homemaker magazines, life trajectories were oriented toward the suburban dream whose aspirants could rest assured that their efforts were appreciated and acknowledged by their peers. Crucially, these relations of recognition were institutionalized at the level of economic and social policy. Keynesian economics, the Fordist model of production with its long-term aims and employment opportunities, as well as comparatively affordable housing constituted central structural aspects underpinning the prevailing conditions for recognition. Put simply, during that time social conditions and the dynamics of recognition converged in a relatively unambiguous normative model for life conduct. Correspondingly, the dynamics of recognition were strongly gendered and thus provided adult recognition for women mainly insofar as they had husbands and cared for the children, on account of the prevalent forms of disrespect to which they were (and often still are) subject. Those on the margins had to rely on forms of recognition within their own milieus for a minimum of self-respect and esteem because their self-identifications and practices were deemed incommensurate with larger societal goals, aspirations, and expectations. For mainstream society in the Golden Age the relations of recognition, and therefore the criteria by which adult status was most explicitly readable, were clear. Standard adulthood was ever more deeply embedded in the culture as a normative ideal; it came to epitomize what being grown up meant.

As discussed in chapter 2, today markers of transition to adulthood have become personalized, subject to individuals' retrospective assignment of significance to their own particular passage to adult status. In other words, these transitions are now deinstitutionalized and therefore no longer constitute markers of adulthood in the narrow sense. In this context it has been proposed that "people are expected to carve out major aspects of their own adulthoods by means of self-directed maturation processes," and that therefore, "adulthood is now more a psychological state than a social status" (Côté 2000: 3). Now, as literature from Rousseau's *Emile* to the German *Bildungsroman* and various studies in adult psychology show, both psychological competencies and social maturity have for long been staple components of adulthood in its social-scientific, cultural, and commonsense representations. In this respect, the central task is to reconcile the personalization of adulthood—growing up as a private endeavor—with the notion that the achievement of adult status relies on *social* (that is, *collective*) recognition. In order to explore this issue, we must investigate "the particular manner in which the mutual granting of recognition is institutionalized," to appropriate Honneth's statement (2003: 138).

We can make first conceptual inroads if we take into consideration the changed exigencies of work and love. The until-further-noticeness that suffuses social relationships in these spheres calls for a maximum of flexibility. The altered terms on which intimate relationships are based contribute their fair share of temporal uncertainty and their own set of insecurities as a trade-off for more equality. These advances in equality are tangibly exemplified in the increasing social recognition of nonsexist attitudes. As for work, long-term careers in one organization are not only very rarely possible, they also no longer attract positive acknowledgement as in the heyday of standard adulthood. On the contrary, the labor market favors those who are flexible, mobile, and willing to change, and thus discriminates against those who want stability and linear, predictable work careers: "The ideal image conveyed by the labour market is that of a completely mobile individual regarding him/herself as a functioning flexible work unit, competitive and ambitious, prepared to disregard the social commitments linked to his/her existence and identity. This perfect employee fits in with the job requirements, prepared to move on whenever necessary" (Beck and Beck-Gernsheim 1995: 6). The commodity market too is a prime mediator between what might be called the supply and demand dynamics of recognition. Weber's (1922) considerations of status as a prime component of social inequality are an early acknowledgement that consumption and consumer lifestyles are important factors of social recognition in modern societies. However, today it is in the daily interactions between consumer demands and supply-side offers that the lines between what are deemed age-appropriate or inappropriate choices are particularly blurred. As we will see in the next chapter, market relationships render the boundaries between adolescent and adult behavior especially fluid.

Both personal troubles and freedoms are contingent on the prevailing dynamics of recognition that serve as cultural guides to life conduct; that help sift that which is cool, fashionable, and popular, appropriate, or normal from those practices deemed uncool, unfashionable, and unpopular, inappropriate, and outside the norm. These conventions largely concern cultural sensibilities—the "presentation of self" and "the arts of impression management" (Goffman 1959)—and are therefore relative to the different social contexts within which individuals operate. In relation to the prevailing structural and cultural conditions, I suggest that there are particular subjective orientations that enhance individuals' chances for social recognition, and especially so for young adults. Thus, those who are willing to "go with the flow," to take each relationship as it comes; who eschew the "till death do us part" promises of old and instead seek, above all, the rewards of mutual personal growth, stand to gain institutional and peer recognition. Those who are willing (and able) to partake of the cultural offerings and material trappings that beckon in our affluent societies as well as those who buy into and embody current masculine and feminine ideals stand to be acknowledged as trendsetters and meet with approving eyes where others go unnoticed.

The more the social imperative of flexibility becomes an internalized quality for individuals, the better are they equipped to deal with the conditions of recognition in various social milieus. The overarching criterion for adult recognition is to be that which society posits as the logical subjective consequence: to be flexible, amenable, and open to change in order to fulfill the exigencies of plural social environments, each one of which may be subject to considerable internal instability and flux. The redefinition of contemporary adulthood and the emergence of the new adulthood can thus be situated in a prevalent fluidity and pluralization of the criteria for recognition concerning a social category that for so long has meant the opposite of flexibility; that has meant—and still connotes—settling down, being at ease with one's place in the world, happy to commit to work and love, ready to take responsibility for oneself and especially for others. Today, individuals' ability to gain recognition is at least partly linked to their competence in negotiating their biographies within a frame of reference that is marked by a "fragility of bonds, . . . in-built transience and 'until-further-noticeness,' coupled with temporariness of commitment and [a] revocability of obligations" (Bauman 2001b: 140).

Reconceptualizing Adulthood

Holtgrewe et al.'s (2000: 18) proposition that rapid social change entails a rupture between "new conditions, new promises and their agents" and old standards is a helpful prompt for a further clarification of the normative lag between the ideals of standard adulthood and social trends. From a recognition-theoretical point of view, there is an ever-present possibility of the development of a lag between those criteria for recognition that are slow in changing and new social conditions and social practices. Holtgrewe and his collaborators (2000: 18) further maintain that it is these old standards against which new situations are measured. Those normative ideals that constituted the criteria for adult recognition at a time when these ideals were commensurate with social practice have come to be incommensurate with present social realities. This tension between norms and practices is the social context for the contemporary trends in question. The implication here is that the normative basis for adulthood is no longer fixed.

The contemporary push toward a redefinition of adulthood can, metaphorically at least, be seen as "a struggle for recognition" that is marked by the assertion of social practice against residual normative ideals. This is not a collective struggle of a self-conscious class of individuals advancing claims for social acknowledgement and validation. Rather, these are unspoken, even unintentional demands on the recognition order—elicitations that flow from everyday engagements with the uncertainties of contemporary modernity. These practices are, if only because of the extent of their critical mass, drivers of social change; drivers of a normative transformation that appears to be headed for a reconciliation of ideals and practices, for the overcoming of the recognition deficit. This implies that if this transformation were to prove successful, the contemporary modalities of adulthood would attain a level of taken-for-grantedness that was for a time accorded to standard adulthood. Yet, as I will elaborate in chapter 4, the trajectories of ideals and practices is asymptotic for reasons that are immanent to modernity. The resolution of normative tensions is set to elude realization.

The relations of social recognition are such that increasingly once-and-for-all attainment of adult status is rarely possible. This is so especially today when ideas concerning how to live and how to act are ambiguous at best. In fact, because individuals move in different milieus and thus need to draw on a variety of competencies, they are apt to elicit and attain recognition in different ways in different social spheres. As Holtgrewe et al. (2000: 13) maintain: "The differentiation of spheres of recognition also means that should individuals experience a recognition deficit in one sphere, they can compensate for this with contrary experiences in another." With regard to adult recognition this can be exemplified thus: individuals may be highly competent at their work as far as the instrumental execution of tasks is concerned and may gain recognition for this, but at the same time be deemed socially inept; they may be considered wonderful parents, while unable to attain employment; they may be married, have a family and a home of their own, but be unable to empathize with their partners and children; or they may be single, childless, unemployed, and live at home, and be a source of inspiration and comfort to their peers.[2]

We may ask here whether this is not an old, familiar situation. The answer is both yes and no. Yes, because competence in the public sphere has never necessarily gone hand in hand with competence in the private sphere. No, because often the force of recognition through the unequivocal acknowledgement of full personhood was such that those deemed responsible adults were for that very reason often in positions of unchallengeable power in the private sphere, and were recognized as such by legislation. Recognition at work, for men at least, was often paralleled by recognition as the sole breadwinner and authority in the home, where, as Erich Fromm (2001: 104) reminds us, "the individual could feel like 'somebody.' He was obeyed by wife and children, he was the center of the stage, and he naively accepted his role as his natural right. He might be a nobody in his social relations, but he was king at home." Also, individuals' exposure to diversity was once relatively limited, and therefore those ways of life that were lived by the majority remained largely uncontested by other claims for recognition, just as the opportunity and necessity to move in very different spheres of recognition too was limited. This has changed markedly over the last several decades. Taking as their starting point recognition at work, Holtgrewe and colleagues (2000: 22) comment on the differentiated nature of the dynamics of recognition: "[E]mployees have disparate experiences of disrespect and recognition in other social spheres: as citizens, lovers, parents, athletes, or as activists in social movements. They experience such disparate forms, standards and reference points of social recognition and have to set priorities in and between them, leave out others, fulfill expectations and defend claims. It appears that precisely this diversity of experiences of social recognition and the tensions between them promotes the dynamics from which struggles for recognition spring."

The discourse around delayed adulthood fails to account for the differentiation of the relations of recognition, and the degree to which the validation of adult status has become fragmented in its reliance on various milieu-specific standards. Rather, certain roles are selected, generalized across the lives of a whole generation, and then equated with immaturity. This allows the identification of an unfinished state of integration because it confuses what individuals do in particular spheres (e.g., prolonged stay in the parental home, late family formation) with individuals' self-identification and stance toward the world per se. Taking Castells's (1997: 7) precept, "identities organize the meaning while roles organize the functions" as our cue, it is evident that the current orthodoxy conflates meaning and function. Moreover, just as the adjective "adolescent" is in common parlance overwhelmingly a pejorative term (Springhall 1984: 20), labels such as adultescents and kidults, and synonymous social-scientific notions, convey the negative connotations that have congealed around the word adolescent. This is but one reason why this perspective requires reconceptualization.

I suggested above that forms of adult recognition have changed from the social validation of modes of life conduct oriented toward certainty, predictability, and long-term planning, to the validation of uncertainty, risk-taking, and short-term projects. I suggested further that those actions and sensibilities that are most attuned to the contingencies of the present and best suited to the contemporary imperative of flexibility stand to reap the rewards of social recognition. By extension, practices that are most conducive to the navigation of uncertain social relations are likely to be reproduced as subjective "rational response[s]" to systemic uncertainty (Bauman 2001a: 52). This is no different when it comes to the specifics of recognition with which I am concerned. Precisely those social trends that are purported to be indicative of a delayed adulthood are highly congruent with contemporary dynamics of adult recognition. In fact, new adults are particularly well integrated in a world that is radically different from the past. The social conditions of the present in interaction with the desires of individuals have helped bring about a radically altered form of adulthood. These relations of recognition, however, are contradictory. Practices may be structurally rewarded while simultaneously being discursively misrecognized as long as the normative ideals of another time remain most readily associated with what it means to be an adult, a full person. To round off the theoretical reconsiderations, the next chapter attends to the ideological dimension of changes in the meaning of contemporary adulthood.

4

FROM ADULTHOOD AS A GOAL
TO YOUTH AS A VALUE

"Americans began by loving youth, and now, out of adult self-pity, they worship it."

Jacques Barzun, The House of Intellect (1959)

The changing relations of adult recognition are linked to the devolution of a teleological notion of adulthood and an ideational expansion of youth. Youth emerges in a new guise; its tropes belong to the ideological underpinning of contemporary adulthood. This is the argument developed in this chapter. To this end, Creedon's (1995: 1) observation is a useful orienting statement: "The Western mind is in love with youth. It is ultimately a hopeless love, a destructive love, a love that is easily exploited. But being love, we are convinced of its nobility, and all warnings against it go unheeded. Nothing can distract our gaze from the freshly minted faces on the magazine cover, the haughty pose of the soccer star, the bared body of the film actress. And this fascination isn't limited to the youthful icons of popular culture; it colors every aspect of Western life, from the family to the workplace." This cultural apotheosis of youth has a long tradition. The image of youth signifying beauty, strength, and vitality goes back to antiquity (Schnapp 1997). Yet, when we think about Creedon's remark that the fascination with this image of youth "colors every aspect of Western life," we are invited to look at youth as more than an aesthetic idea, as something that is intrinsic to Western societies' self-understanding, and individuals' orientation to life: the emergence of youth as a lifestyle for all ages. This transformation in the history of youth affects the meaning of adulthood.

Adolescents, Teenagers, and Youth Culture

This chapter variously refers to adolescence, youth, and teenagers. I begin with a clarification of adolescence and youth. The notion of the teenager will be explored separately. Analytic distinction is all the more necessary because there is considerable conflation of these terms in the literature. For example, Fornäs and Bolin (1995: 3) state: "Youth is, on the one hand, a physiological development phase, commencing in puberty and ending when the body has more or less finished growing. On the other hand, it is a psychological life phase extending through the different phases of adolescence and post-adolescence." Some historians follow suit and remark that youth is "situated somewhere between the shifting margins of infantile dependency and adult autonomy" (Levi and Schmitt 1997). From this view youth is a transitional category. At the same time, commonsense connotations of youth generally posit it as an attribute. This youth, just like the beauty with which it is often associated, is in the eye of the beholder. One can have entered deep old age and be "young at heart," have a "young mind," even a youthful appearance "for one's age." For someone in their eighties, a person in their fifties is most certainly still young.

Although youth was understood to be a stage of life in earlier periods of European history (Levi and Schmitt 1997; Heywood 2001), it took on special significance as a transitionary phase between childhood and adulthood with the increasing affluence of the bourgeoisie from about the late eighteenth century (Gillis 1981; May and von Prondczynsky 1991; Hanawalt 1992; Mitterauer 1992; Boëthius 1995; Furstenberg 2000). In the course of the nineteenth century youth came to denote that period of life which, for those (males, at first) who had the necessary means, was devoted to an increasingly prolonged period of education. Separated from the world of work and thus to some extent isolated from the world of adults, these bourgeois youths came to inhabit a sphere of their own in which they were relatively sheltered from the rapidly industrializing domain of work. Changed social circumstances have made mid-nineteenth-century bourgeois youth an adolescent prototype. Century's end brought the social scientific legitimation required to render adolescence an institutionalized life phase of its own.

In the meantime, the relative isolation of middle and upper-class young men from adults also helped imbue the idea of youth with a romantic myth of naturalness, simplicity, and freedom; it came to signify a period of "renewal of the certainties of life that seemed buried in the world of divided labour and 'materialism'" (Trommler 1985: 15). This "utopia of natural life" (Trommler 1985: 33), freed from the cares of the adult world, had little to do with the experiences of working-class youth. In fact, the simultaneous existence of two ways of being young—one spent in educational institutions, the other in workshops, in factories, on the farm—came to signify a distinction that attracted the attention of educators, reformers, and the emerging expert class of youth workers: that between the bourgeois model youth and the precocious working-class lad (Gillis 1981). That this perceived precocity was a matter of economic survival for the lower socioeconomic order—one of the keys to working-class resistance to education— does not appear to have affected common perceptions (von Trotha 1982: 259).

Despite the distinctly different experiences of youth, a uniform image began to emerge from about the end of the nineteenth century, holding sway over succeeding decades. Two main factors for this can be singled out. First, education increasingly became a general condition for the betterment of individuals' life chances in a changing economic environment. Particularly with the emergence of white-collar jobs, education furnished the very real possibility of social mobility, providing a growing number of youth with the opportunity to transcend their class (Gillis 1981: 119; 168–70; von Trotha 1982: 260). Class-segregated educational institutions notwithstanding, the experience of a relatively prolonged education gradually became universal. As a result, the experiential differences between childhood and adulthood also increased for most individuals (Gillis 1981: 108–10; Mitterauer 1992: 24–25; Heywood 2001: 25). Second, in the wake of this development, the behavioral and biological sciences came to agree upon a common view under which young people's status could be subsumed: the special physical and psychological nature of the developing person (Gillis 1981; von Trotha 1982; Mitterauer 1992). The specific way in which young people's experiences, behaviors, and attitudes came to be represented amounted to a significant redefinition of youth, which particularly reduced the preadult phase of life "to an object of scientific observation and clinical treatment by adults" (Gillis 1981: 142). This reconceptualization shaped everyday and social scientific perceptions of and attitudes toward young people, whose development became a matter of some urgency: "What mattered was finding ways of turning the immature, irrational, incompetent, asocial and acultural child into a mature, rational, competent, social and autonomous adult" (Heywood 2001: 3). Generalized across barriers of class and gender through education and a growing number of youth organizations (e.g., the Boy Scouts), this approach became constitutive for a particular perspective on youth: adolescence.

In the social sciences, adolescence essentially denotes a phase of psychological and physiological development between childhood and adulthood. The age-range for which this applies is unclear. While the Oxford English Dictionary does not represent a reference text of developmental psychology, it nevertheless reflects broad views. The authors pitch the age span of adolescence at "14 to 25 in males," and "12 to 21 in females" (1989: 170). Others note that "roughly 9 to 14" for both girls and boys is an acceptable standard (McDonald 1996: 1), while the U.S. Society for Adolescent Medicine defines adolescence as stretching from 10 to 26 years of age (Furedi 2003: 4). As shown in chapter 1, terms such as "postadolescence" considerably extend this phase of development, leading some to include the early thirties in the adolescent bracket. But age and notions of development are not sufficient to outline the concept of adolescence. As Hanawalt (1992: 343) reminds us, "[m]odern Western Europe did not invent adolescence, but it did alter its definition." While biological development is an anthropological constant, the way in which this phase is accommodated by society is historically and culturally specific, and thus our conception of adolescence is unique to Western societies, a point made most prominently by Margaret Mead (1928). Adolescence is but an aspect of youth, albeit an aspect in its historical transformation that is far-reaching in its consequences for present perceptions of and attitudes toward young people. Emphasis on behavioral and psychological development coupled with the social realities (e.g., relative economic dependence) that confront adolescents because of their "special" developmental status, renders the notion of adolescence more specific than the more general notion of youth. In a sense, then, adolescence has supplanted youth as a category, while youth like "young," is retained in our cultural understanding and vocabulary as an attribute.

The prominence of adolescence can be understood as arising from twin processes of differentiation and homogenization that began in the nineteenth century and continued throughout the twentieth. Differentiation here denotes the consolidation of institutional arrangements that served to segregate the young from the adult. At the same time, a certain homogenization of young people as a category of individuals with specific physiological and psychological needs was effected under the term adolescence. These are different processes insofar as differentiation occurred on the structural level—the reflections of which were captured by theorists such as Parsons (1942a; 1942b)—while homogenization refers to how adolescents were perceived and explained. Just as the differentiation of young people was elevated to taken-for-granted status through the institutionalization of formal age categories (e.g., age-graded education), so homogenization was given scientific legitimacy through the psychologization of the growing person. These processes heightened the possibilities for social control over young people while keeping power asymmetries between adults and the young intact (Musgrove 1964; Gillis 1981; von Trotha 1982; Bourdieu 1993). Viewed from the perspective of social integration, these historical developments also amount to an alignment of young people's life trajectories with the burgeoning system of industrial production. To use the language of current life course research and youth studies, the differentiation and homogenization of young people helped establish "pathways" to adulthood, at least for those who had the chance to take advantage of educational opportunities. It is during this period that we see the emergence of the institutionalized life course, as discussed in chapter 2.

However, these integrative processes also strengthened the view that those young people who did not follow the norm were deviant. The social construction of the juvenile delinquent was a significant step toward this end. Adolescence came to be the locus of an immaturity whose specificities were causally connected to delinquency. Indeed, cultural sensibilities were such that even the slightest deviance from what was considered normal, such as "irregular language," was seen as deviant behavior and an indication of the beginnings of delinquency (Passerini 1997: 326). For example, in the mid-twentieth-century United States—the same time and place that grew standard adulthood—concerns and suspicions about young people fomented institutional responses at the highest level, as exemplified by the establishment of the Youth Correction Division (1951), the Senate Subcommittee on Juvenile Delinquency (1953), the Division of Juvenile Delinquency (1954), and the Committee on Youth Employment (1961). The burgeoning concern with juvenile delinquency in that era was connected to another complementary fact. During this time a particular image of what it meant to be young emerged: the teenager. In this idea leisure pursuits and adolescent characteristics were conflated and came to represent a norm that allowed so-called delinquent or deviant behaviors to come into relief.

The teenager of the 1950s can be viewed as the high point in the development of adolescence as envisaged by generations of educators and youth workers. There are at least two factors that contributed to the formation of this kind of youth: one was postwar affluence, the other unique demographic circumstances. Much of young people's identification with peers, such as personal appearance and leisure pursuits, depends on their spending capacity. These identifications play a vital role in their subcultural differentiation from adults.[1] But the very dependence of youth culture on a separation from the adult world was (and is) underpinned by their relative isolation from the sphere of work and/or opportunities to earn a full adult wage. Working-class youth who were much closer to if not part of the world of grown-ups, had from about the end of the nineteenth century come to be seen as precocious. By the 1950s they were trendsetters; but only insofar as they represented the dangerous side of youth: theirs was a social milieu that was considered most conducive to delinquency and derived its rebellious glamour in part from the very distance from what was considered the teenage world proper: "the world of high school and homework" (Hine 1999: 226).

After the Second World War, teenagers emerged largely by virtue of their parents' affluence, across all strata of society. But in order for parents to be willing to support the leisure pursuits by which teenagers were mainly identified, something else had to change: the affective relationship between parents and children. Here, changes in the demographic makeup of Western societies cannot be underestimated. While the Australian case is perhaps not as spectacular as the North American case, it is nevertheless typical. Following the Second World War here as in other Western societies the baby boom occurred. This unique demographic trend was not marked by women having more children, but by the fact that more women married, that they did so at younger ages, and that they were thus likely to have children in their twenties (Gilding 2000: 205). Relative affluence meant that attention to children's wants as well as needs became economically possible for the majority. Also, the sheer number of children and young mothers made child raising an issue of great priority and ushered in a "regime of permissiveness," especially when compared to the parent–child relationships of preceding generations (Bittman and Pixley 1997: 56).

The baby boom teenagers were numerous and thus highly visible, and by the late 1950s began to attract the attention of marketing and advertising professionals who connected developmental theories to market behavior and helped produce a unified and strongly normative image of the young person. This is particularly evident in the case of teenage girls. Having discovered a teenage consumer with "particular needs and desires determined by age and biology," media and advertising discourse began to center on the fulfillment of traditional gendered caregiver roles that were to be supplemented by pretensions to glamour and charm (Johnson 1989). Apart from the obvious benefits to commerce, consumption provided young people with the possibility to exercise a degree of choice according to taste and so to identify with other teenagers: "The market suggested that they were not to be confined to this child's world but could occupy a whole world of their own. The market would provide them with their own clothes, hairstyles, music, radio programs, popular literature and their own magazines. Thus young people, the market suggested, could be in control of their own growing up" (Johnson 1989: 9). Such lifestyle differentiation situated teenagers more completely outside the adult world than was previously the case, heightening youth's self-awareness in the process. While on the one hand this brought with it a measure of social and moral independence from parents manifest in a more overt turn to peers for approbation, on the other hand it intensified adults' perception of young people as both different from themselves and homogeneous as a group. For decades to come, social scientists were to be concerned with what Coleman (quoted in Passerini 1997: 320) identified as a "youth sub-culture in industrial society" that spoke "a different language." In Britain, this concern reached its zenith in the 1970s and continued through to the late 1980s with the Centre of Contemporary Cultural Studies' (the "Birmingham School") focus on such youth subcultures as the Teddy Boys, Mods, Rockers, Skinheads, Punks, and New Romantics, to name but a few (Hall and Jefferson 1976). The emerging recognition of young people's otherness, besides constituting attempts to understand the great diversity of the "youth question" (Cohen 1997), allowed the social scientist to dabble in a form of ethnography that was more like an intrasocietal anthropology in order to mine the rich seams of another culture without having to embark on journeys into distant lands.

The two outstanding theorists of the postwar period who attempted to explain the difference of teenagers were Talcott Parsons and Erik Erikson. Parsons's (1942a; 1942b) account of youth culture situates it within the shifting value orientations that underwrite society in the transformation from premodernity to modernity. Family socialization along traditional patriarchal lines comes up against the increasing differentiation of social roles and their rationalized, market-oriented organization. The family is divested of its socializing functions amid the increasing segregation of the young from the adult world of work. Parsons's account is an early sociological formulation of adolescence as a moratorium from responsibility, a period after childhood, but before adulthood. Erikson brought ego-psychology to his analysis of the "life cycle." As such he is, to this day, perhaps the central theorist elaborating the connection between adolescence and identity formation and, more particularly, "identity crisis." Erikson takes Hall's account of development to its logical conclusion: the life cycle as a whole is divided into discrete life stages, each with its own set of polarities that constitute the tension between ego and culture (Erikson 1950). Although incorporating cultural and historical mediations, Erikson's approach is an important example of the tendency to treat young people in a homogenizing fashion, that is, as adolescents with innate biological and cognitive traits and propensities typical of a particular phase of human development.

Young people's orientation toward their own peer group—a turn to like-minded others that was fostered by cultural representations (rock 'n' roll and teenflix with their idols, the drive-in, teen fashion)—came soon to be seen as evidence of what Riesman (1950) diagnosed as modern individuals' "other-directedness." Applied to adolescence—as it was in Friedenberg's *The Vanishing Adolescent* (1964), the second edition for which Riesman wrote an introduction—Riesman's study of conformity and individuality in postwar North America can be summed up thus: in a period of a person's life when identity formation is seen as *the* crucial project, external sources of identification and self-verification (the media, peers) take the place of an active engagement with the world in terms of socially fixed values acquired through primary socialization ("inner-directedness"). For social scientists and psychologists such as Friedenberg, consumption and conformity came to be seen as sources of a passivity that threatened to vanquish adolescence as it was known. The emergence of the counterculture seemed to put an end to these speculations. By the late 1960s and into the 1970s the meaning of youth underwent another transformation, one that was to reverberate decades into the future—and it resonates, in crucial ways, with the cultural environment and social trends of the present.

Counterculture: Adolescents as Self-Conscious Social Actors

The politicization of young people in the wake of the Civil Rights movement and the Vietnam War, as well as the May days of Paris and Italy's "long hot summer," effected a shift in middle-class young people's self-awareness, in their relationships with the parent generation, and thus with standard adulthood. *New York Press* editor John Strausbaugh (2001: 13) reminisces: "Whereas some '50s teens might have felt alienated from their parents, many '60s and '70s teens were downright alien to them. . . . Indeed, between the long hair, the drugs, the rock, the free love, the pacifism, the no-work-ethic embrace of poverty, the flirtations with Eastern mysticism, and the radical politics, a subset of young people in the '60s came to be identified as inhabiting a completely separate culture from that of their parents."

The "culture industry," in Adorno's sense (2002), continued to profit from this "emergence of the adolescent as self-conscious social actor" (Hobsbawm 1995: 325). This phase in the historical trajectory of youth rendered it a category that surpassed marketers' expectations, and one without which consumer capitalism in its present form is unthinkable. The teenagers of the late 1940s and 1950s could be sold the consumer products that helped them conform to standards of behavior, to be popular with the peer group, even to mimic the "rebel without a cause" of James Dean's and Marlon Brando's type. But the counterculture proved even more lucrative from a marketing perspective: youths' "revolt" against "the system" could be sold back to them as pop-cultural artifacts just as easily as their turn to love (free, universal, or otherwise). And so, in the mid 1960s Madison Avenue admen in a "frenzy for hip" exchanged their gray flannel suits for the psychedelic accoutrements and lifestyles of the counterculture (Frank 1997: 109).

The emergence of the rock star is a phenomenon worth considering in this context. Although the idol of the 1960s and 1970s was prefigured by the (always male) rebel of the 1950s, whose autonomy was all the more appealing the more it appeared to transgress the espoused values of the parent generation, the likes of Janis Joplin, Jimi Hendrix, Jim Morrison, Brian Jones, and others had no equivalent in the earlier history of youth. Not just their work assured them immortality, but their premature deaths, which came to embody mottos that stood for a whole generation: to be here "not for a long time, but a good time," "tutto e subito," and so forth (Hobsbawm 1995: 324). Death itself became an imaginary lifestyle orientation. For the vast majority of young people this orientation remained of course unrealized. Thus, having lived beyond their teens and on into their twenties and thirties, they transformed the motto "die while you are young" into a precept that, as an idea, holds sway today: be young till you die.

Beginning in the 1960s and 1970s youth began to shed part of its image, that part that denoted it as a preparatory phase for adulthood. Aspects of youth— particularly those characteristics that are associated with youthfulness—came to compete with standard adulthood and came to be seen as the aim of human development. Today, young people have lost the foil against which they were, for a time, to rebel, against which their "deviance" could come into relief. Instead, youth sequestered from connotations of adolescence has become an ideology for life per se. It has, however, neither replaced nor challenged adulthood as such, nor has the expansion of youth become synonymous with a prolonged adolescence or delayed adulthood. Rather, it has become both an important factor in the redefinition of adulthood and a central ideological component of its new modalities.

The Expansion of Youth and the New Adulthood

At the core of the expansion of youth lies a selective and contradictory societal sanctioning of its socially constructed qualities. While on the one hand youth as a way of life is promulgated as desirable in today's flexible world, the ascribed characteristics of adolescence are seen as undesirable and to be left behind. The ideal is to be adult and youthful but not adolescent: to be open to change, but responsibly so; to be willing to live in the present only, but to invest in a secure future; to be mature, but not settled; to improvise, but know what you want—to be adult and eschew settling down. Berger's (1966: 69) conception of maturity as "the state of mind that has settled down, come to terms with the status quo, given up the wilder dreams of adventure and fulfillment," so indicative of the time during which he wrote his treatise, is at least in part no longer appropriate. Experimental attitudes toward life and dreams of adventure are today no longer contrary to the status quo, but an imperative component of it.

Liminality Without Limits

The social imperatives of the new adulthood can be further conceptualized by drawing on van Gennep's (1960) notion of liminality. According to van Gennep, "rites of passage" are marked by a trajectory from "separation" from one stage to "aggregation" with the next, while liminality is the in-between phase. With respect to the transition to adulthood, youth has been called a "liminal stage": being "neither here nor there," neither child nor adult, youth is often perceived as a state of incompleteness (Turner 1974: 232). Being neither here nor there, youthful liminality also means that in a world of no promises, in which the possibilities for long-term self-projections are increasingly foreclosed, young people acquire a natural attitude of a kind that prepares them to have few expectations beyond the present, to make no commitments beyond the immediate future. Furthermore, affinities between structural conditions and cultural ideals of personal growth radically alter the meaning of liminality. Western individuals' fascination with personal development permeates contemporary discourse. A visit to the airport bookshop, the most cursory glance at TV talk shows, the perusal of popular magazines, the burgeoning field of life coaching, conversations with friends, acquaintances, and family, questions fielded at job interviews (e.g., "How would this position enrich your life?"), will confirm that personal growth in one form or another is a dominant cultural theme. The spirit of Romanticism with its insistence on an essential self legitimated by Jungian psychology has, it seems, finally found the necessary market conditions to flourish as a mass cultural form.

This trend can be connected to contemporary perceptions of an open-ended future as well as the reality and perception of proliferating options. As discussed in chapter 2, the perception of a profusion of options helps assuage existential anxieties. At the same time, individuals feel the need to narrow the options in order to make the world more comprehensible. The belief in individual choice, and the belief in one's capacity to choose should one decide to do so, is part of a psychological reservoir that is drawn upon to retain the belief in one's agency. Anything is possible, it seems, as long as you put your mind to it. But this also means something else: many of life's options are deferrable, able to be put on hold until further notice. Moreover, no choice need be final; all choices appear in principle revocable. Research findings showing that many young people across all borders of gender, ethnicity, and class are largely optimistic about the road ahead (e.g., Du Bois-Reymond 1998; Arnett 2000b; Dwyer and Wyn 2001) can therefore be linked to an internalization of unbounded possibilities, the actualization of which is subject to individual resolve. At the same time, this is an indication that the ability of young people to actively connect their own destinies with the social forces that shape them is diminishing.

In a like fashion, the repudiation or at least scant awareness of social constraints supports the so-called postmaterialist attitudes attributed to young people (Inglehart 1977; 1990). The actualization of options is individualized, and personal development becomes a modus vivendi. When the idea of personal growth in its various forms becomes both an espoused and an action-orienting value, making once-and-for-all decisions about life, such as settling down or choosing a career, makes as little sense as deciding that you have grown enough, that you have finally realized your self, reached your full potential, and so forth. Youth in the sense of adolescence with its promise of resolution in standard adulthood, no longer obtains for many individuals:

> What emerges clearly is a rupture with the model of youth that developed in industrial society, where youth was a structured transition from childhood to adulthood, organized around a series of stages such as moving into permanent employment and a stable relationship and ultimately establishing a new household. That social and cultural model of youth focused on the future; it was one where youth was lived as a 'project.' That model is now profoundly disorganized. The clear temporal stages which shaped it have been 'desynchronized' to the point that youth is no longer lived as a project defined in terms of the future, but more as a 'condition,' no longer associated with images of the future (McDonald 1999: 3).

At the same time, to be young (at heart) matters precisely because the future is still open. The future matters—and all the more so because it lacks definition. Consequently, youth as a liminal stage takes on a meaning that goes beyond the transitional qualities attributed to adolescence. When in addition to the perception of an open future and too many options the interminable process of striving for personal growth becomes a goal, adulthood can no longer retain its status as final destination; it is replaced by youth as a value. In other words, the liminality attributed to youth (adolescence) is becoming a quality of contemporary adult-hood. But this is not to be equated with a prolonged adolescence, nor with a delayed adulthood, for this kind of liminality is in one important respect at vari-ance with van Gennep's notion. Van Gennep's concept presupposes two states that border the liminal phase: a state that has been left behind, and another that is not yet reached. The liminality of the new adulthood, however, knows no limit. Thus, while standard adulthood as the classic resolution to the liminality of adolescence remains as a normative model, the actual practices of contem-porary young adults render the new adulthood liminal without limits. This is congruent with the fluid dynamics of recognition in the present era—dynamics in the constitution of which the market plays a significant role.

The Expansion of Youth and Social Recognition

By the 1950s the metaphysics of youth, with its origins in antiquity and revital-ized in nineteenth-century Romanticism, had encountered its twentieth-century realization. First in the United States, then in other Anglophone societies, and finally in continental Europe, where the echoes of war delayed economic growth and the generalization of affluence across classes, advertising agents and mar-keters set out not only to harness what was perceived to be young people's cre-ative potentials by either employing or emulating them, but also to capitalize on greater affluence and the corresponding demand for youth-specific commodities. This also meant that the marketing profession itself underwent changes, "for the successful entrepreneurs of youth subculture had themselves to be flexible and adventurous, youthful in outlook and, increasingly, in actual years" (Marwick 1999: 42). Most importantly, segments of the market recognized and exploited an attitude of what was to become the driving force of a booming culture industry: young people's aversion to anything grown-up, mainstream, or reminiscent of "the establishment." Through music and its promulgation on proliferating record labels, radio and television shows, and magazines, and its affinities with particular fashions and lifestyles, the culture industry not only expressed but also promoted and directed what being young meant.

The tropes and ideology of youthfulness—élan and verve, flexibility and mobility, risk-taking and experimenting propensities, creativity and thirst for change, situational living and present-centeredness, cutting-edge know-how, up-to-dateness, and beauty—are not only understood as desirable in their embodied sense; they are also cast as desirable, if not imperative, from the standpoint of businesses and corporations of all kinds. For one, the increasing relaxation of what counts as age-appropriate consumption behavior nurtures people's sense of proliferating options regarding self-presentation. Tastes for fashion, music, elec-tronic gadgetry, and leisure pursuits need no longer necessarily take their cues from the teenage/adult binary. From a marketing perspective this means that the profitable leanings of teens, with small product and advertising modifications, also apply to older—even much older—age cohorts. Market share thus potentially increases as the target group becomes larger: "Teen tastes have become the tastes of all because the economic system requires this to be so. . . . In a phrase, youth sells!" (Danesi 2003: ix)

The social conditions of contemporary life are to a much greater extent commensurate with the expansion of youth than was the case during the three decades after the Second World War. Work and private life provide further impetus for adults' emulation of youth's qualities. When long-term fulltime employment is fast becoming a thing of the past and a growing percentage of working people fill positions in precarious temporary or part-time employment; when (partly as a consequence) future time horizons contract; and when institutionalized commitments between intimates are freed from normative constraints, then flexibility, openness to change, risk-taking attitudes, and present-centeredness constitute not only an elective affinity with structural and cultural exigencies, but the internalization, and hence a normalization, of a stance toward work, intimate relationships, and life in general. It is in this context that historian Pierre Nora's (1992: 510) view acquires particular poignancy: "Youth . . . has emancipated itself from the sociological reality of being a social minority and even freed itself from the symbolism of age to become an organizing principle for society as a whole, a mental image that guides the distribution of roles and positions, an end unto itself."

Others argue along similar lines from a perspective that is highly critical of Western trends. In a society that is unable to come to terms with the natural deterioration of the human body as part of the aging process, a "cult of youth" is said to have gained prevalence (e.g., Lasch 1979: 207–17). "To make matters worse," writes Côté (2000: 49), "the media and mass marketers have exploited for profit this obsession with youth. Those who are susceptible to such influences have attempted to maintain their youth as dictated by the profiteers." Côté's critique supports the proposition that the contemporary expansion of youth is qualitatively different from age-old desires to prolong youth's physical attributes. The devolution of standard adulthood in terms of young people's practices and orientations is inextricably bound up with the market's perpetuation of discontent. Businesses and corporations—be they sellers, marketers, or advertisers—have become principal mediators in the supply and demand structures of social recognition. They contribute to the blurring of the boundaries between life stages and benefit from the fragmentation of once-linear, institutionally shored up life trajectories insofar as they posit individuals as seekers of recognition. In this process market transactions are presented and valued as ideal. The confluence of market prerogatives and the need to be recognized as a full person is underwritten by a particular aspect of Western societies' conceptions of the good life:

> Whereas . . . political liberalism assumes that we should choose our individual conceptions of the good life or our 'comprehensive doctrines' [Rawls] of the good freely and authentically, and consequently in a very pluralistic manner, capitalism requires for its survival that we do *not* make use of the whole range of options that are legally, within the political framework, open to us, but choose our conceptions from the narrow and specific range of options that are congenial to, or compatible with, the systematic imperatives of capitalism. Only if the vast majority of people view themselves primarily as consumers and producers, and consequently direct their energies and aspirations toward professional careers on the one hand and ever increasing consumption on the other . . . can growth-dependent capitalist societies sustain themselves. (Rosa 1998a: 202–03, original emphasis)

It stands to reason that individuals' realization of what the good life means to them has historically been expected to take place during adulthood, a time when central questions about individuals' biographies are supposed to be resolved and adult recognition attained. Consumption practices, just like work, are thus entwined in the attainment of adult status. We gain a glimpse of this phenomenon in *Things* (1990), Georges Perec's first novel. The author draws a picture of the subtle transformation in consumption practices that accompanies his protagonists' self-definition as adults, a process that is linked to the culturally bound exigencies of materialism. In this excerpt, Jerome and Sylvie's desire for the good life is awakening; and it is one that neatly corresponds to modern capitalist relations of recognition:

> Those were the years when they wandered endlessly around Paris. They would stop at every antique dealer's. They would go into department stores and stay for hours on end, marveling and already scared but not daring to admit it to themselves, not daring to face squarely that particular type of despicable voracity which was to become their fate, their raison d'être, their watchword, for they were still marveling at and almost drowning under the scale of their own needs, of the riches laid out before them, of the abundance on offer. . . .
> . . . And so, step by step, as they took their place in the real world in a rather deeper way than in the past when, as the children of middle-class families of no substance and then as undifferentiated students without individual form, they had had but a superficial and skimpy view of the world, that is how they began to grasp what it meant to be a person of standing.
> This concluding revelation, which, strictly speaking, was not a revelation at all but the culmination of the long-drawn-out process of their social and psychological maturing, and of which they would not have been able to describe the steps without a great deal of difficulty, put the final touch on their metamorphosis. (1990: 42–43)

This drift toward the actualization of personhood, to become "a person of standing" through the imagining and acquisition of a consumer lifestyle indicates the extent to which this cultural ideal is internalized. Commensurate with my argument, this is, in fact, the internalization of existing dynamics of adult recognition. Individuals' realization of the good life cannot be divorced from the collective understanding of what it entails. Thus, the classic markers of adulthood were for a time closely linked to a specific conception of what it meant to lead a good (i.e., socially validated) existence. However pluralized such notions appear to be today, the market serves here as a kind of focusing entity. This in turn means that ultimately the range of options concerning the good life is predominantly one of consumer choices, which implies further that contemporary relations of adult recognition are embedded in the dynamism of market capitalism:

> As research in this field has clearly shown, we do not define our conceptions of the good life autonomously; we always depend on the fact that we want to be recognized, and consequently we depend on what we are recognized for in our culture. Since individuals can only get the recognition they need if they, at least to some extent, productively and creatively acquire and internalize the central values of society, and since they (as Hegel pointed out) in turn must value those by whom they want to be recognized, the perpetuation and reproduction of collective definitions of the good life seems to be ensured. The dialectics of recognition thus might even be the main reason for the absence of an extensive pluralization of conceptions of the good life, which, according to the doctrines of political liberalism, should already be a social reality. (Rosa 1998a: 207)

It follows that the realization of the good life in accordance with the relations of adult recognition that prevailed under the social conditions of the postwar era is no longer possible. While work and consumption promise to fulfill the need for recognition as full members of society, the *actual* satisfaction of this need is the antithesis of market dynamics whose very momentum relies on individuals' dissatisfaction. This dissatisfaction is nurtured by a perception of proliferating options promising the possibility of betterment based on the centrality of personal growth as an existential axiom. The difficulties in realizing the self and the modern impossibility to die "satiated with life," go hand in hand. Thus, the emergence of new norms of adulthood takes place under dynamics of recognition that are fluid and ambiguous—as fluid, that is, as the contingencies of supply and demand, and as ambiguous as the aim of self-realization. Under these conditions a reconciliation of ideal and practice akin to the standard adulthood of the Golden Age is destined to remain an interminable work in progress.

The Market and the Blurring of Boundaries

Commonsense boundaries between life stages begin to blur to the degree to which the market liberates patterns of consumption from the constraints of age norms. We may think here about department stores that offer thongs and padded bras for preteens and adults alike (*Daily Telegraph* 2002), about six-year-olds who worry about their body image, and about child beauty pageants (Giroux 2000). We may consider the commodification of children's games while those more au-tonomous forms of play devoid of coaches, umpires, and adult cheer squads are disappearing (Postman 1982: 4). Concerning the changing nature of work, we may refer to eight-year-olds who choose school subjects according to career con-siderations (*Sydney Morning Herald* 2001b); to unemployed teenagers who after years of balancing school and employment "work for the dole";[2] to individuals in their thirties who start yet another temporary job; and to people in their fifties who sit university exams, while others of similar age are made (or are given the opportunity) to learn how to dress for job interviews by employment agencies after thirty years in gainful employment. As youth expands and becomes an ethic of life per se, the historical trajectory of youth is undergoing a reversal of sorts: from differentiation to de-differentiation.

In the aesthetic sphere there are other explicit signs of de-differentiation, and perhaps in none more so than those genres of music that are heavily vested with generational and age-coded representations. The recycling of pop music is one aspect of this intergenerational process. Remixes of hits from previous decades both cater to the nostalgic sentiments of individuals who were teens in the periods in which the original material first came to market, and at the same time respond to and shape the cultural sensibilities of the successor gen-eration. Another instance is the phenomenon of rock stars who despite their biological aging continue to "perform" their youth. Once doyens of the young in their own youth, and once imbued with antiestablishment élan, the likes of Mick Jagger (b. 1949) and Keith Richards (b. 1943) of the Rolling Stones, Pete Townshend (b. 1946) and Roger Daltrey (b. 1944) of The Who, Jonny Rotten (b. 1956) of the self- and industry-styled anarchic Sex Pistols, and many of their colleagues, continue to grace concert stages around the world. For critics such as John Strausbaugh (2001), they have long lost the type of credibility once attributed to them by press, peers, and fans; a credibility that was anchored in rock as the quintessential cultural form framing and giving expression to what it meant to be young in Western culture. Having outlived the promise to die young and thus to live forever, today these pop icons are little more than living sites of memory that link those who have biologically outgrown adolescence to their teenage years.

It could be argued that Mick Jagger and Keith Richards cut unusual figures in outfits styled for people forty years their juniors, and that it appears absurd for The Who to continue to sing the self-referential "The Kids are Alright" and "My Generation" (containing the much-seized-upon phrase "Hope I die before I get old"). Such sentiments are testimony to the fact not only that informal age norms still have considerable force, but that the normative ideal of standard adulthood persists. Responding to Strausbaugh's notion that rock is and ought to be "youth music," Ellen Willis (quoted in Strausbaugh 2001: 120) maintains: "I think you're framing the problem backwards. The problem is that in American culture . . . there's this idea that grownup [sic] people are supposed to 'settle down.' We're supposed to be interested in work and family, period. We're not supposed to have any sort of communal culture beyond that. We're certainly not supposed to have any communal culture of which eroticism and intensity of feeling are really important." Aerosmith guitarist John Perry expresses his own internalization of the cultural pressures to conform to ideals of adult behavior and highlights both the normative power and the ambiguity of standard adulthood in our present circumstances: "I was about 35 when it hit me. Is this any way for an adult to behave? What kind of role model am I to my kids? Does this mean anything? I felt stranded" (*LA Times* 2002).

Our "love with youth" is not confined to the "youthful icons of popular culture" (Creedon 1995: 1). The ideology of youth is, for example, readily connected to the imperative of flexibility in the labor market, where it underwrites the supply of human resources who are open to change and thus apt to be malleable to structural fluctuations—sifting out, in the process, those over-forties who are deemed "too old" (e.g. *Ehrenreich* 2005). With respect to consumption, the parameters of recognition are now shifting as commonsense knowledge about age-appropriate practices is tending toward more openness. The metamorphosis experienced by the protagonists of Perec's novel may today be even harder to locate than it was in the 1960s, the novel's time of reference. As consumer behavior is becoming less and less subject to social opprobrium, current market conditions appear to democratize the life course. But this loosening of prescription concerning what is deemed age-appropriate and inappropriate is counteracted by the symbolic prescriptions of advertising promising recognition subject to the right purchase.

Just as the identification of adolescents through social scientific and market processes led to young people's integration into the industrial system, so the contemporary intergenerational de-differentiation and expansion of youth effects individuals' integration into society under the prevailing conditions of uncertainty. From the standpoint of the market, de-differentiation, just like yesterday's differentiation, leads to homogenization as the plethora of choices and options appear now to be open to all. But there is a qualitative difference: the market driven homogenization of today is manifest in the degree to which the differences between the marketable demographics childhood, youth, and adulthood are smoothed over. Thus Creedon, referring specifically to the United States, has a point when he remarks that "American culture," whose icons and representations are more than familiar to other Westerners, "has a peculiar leveling effect on the generations" (1995: 1). For those who most directly benefit from commodity and labor market conditions the expansion of youth is good news, especially with respect to the post-1970 generation. This generation was born contingent and lacks the social memory of a time when different social conditions prevailed. Its members have therefore been socialized into and have interiorized modes of life that are most conducive to the market processes of contemporary modernity. Their performance as market actors has to a large extent determined the degree of social recognition they have been able to attain. At the same time, systemically induced dissatisfaction ensures that the quest for recognition in the marketplace remains interminable. This, again, fits hand in glove with the centrality of personal growth as a potentially unending process of individuation.

As "youthfulness . . . has become the signature of a whole culture" (Lenzen 1991: 45), the tropes of youthfulness constitute an overarching value in themselves, and perhaps especially for those who have outgrown its biological delimitations. And it is in a specific sense that youth as a value is today coming to replace adulthood as a goal: the expansion of youth is one ideological aspect supporting contemporary processes of adult recognition. It is central to the prevailing recognition deficit (chapter 3). While those aspects of youth that are mythologized as beauty, strength, vitality, carefreeness, and malleability, and as penchants for improvising and risk-taking underpin the *structural* social recognition of the new adulthood, the same attributes are at the core of the *discourse* that posits young people as trapped in a perpetual adolescence—a discourse that ignores the social conditions under which coming of age occurs for many today.

The enactments of youth as elaborated here have become possible because, at least in principle, the highly differentiated market has enveloped the core constituent of the contemporary dynamics of recognition—flexibility in all spheres of life—in a dream of long cultural standing: individuals' desire for youthfulness. To an extent, the market individualizes systemic conditions because the ideology of youth has become naturalized in the context of systemic and cultural demands. That is not to say that contemporary young adults are helpless victims to market forces; nor do I intend to subscribe to an undue economic reductionism. It is merely to point out that it is amid these social and economic exigencies that their constitution of a new adulthood takes place; it is simply to acknowledge and to reaffirm that capitalist exchange relations do indeed have a bearing on self-identification and therefore need to be taken into account. That failing, much social research concerning changing ideas and practices, and particularly the changing exigencies of the life course, can only be of limited adequacy. With this caveat in mind, I now turn to new adults' articulations of experiences, views, and perceptions.

5

New Adult Voices I:
The Meaning of Adulthood

$$\approx\!\!\!\gg\!\!\!\ll\!\!\!\approx$$

"Adulthood? It's a state of mind."

Karen

The preceding chapters have put the case that today the "how" and "what" of adulthood are indeterminate and that this is, among other things, contingent upon the diminishing possibilities to envision, let alone plan, long-term life trajectories. Thus, turning to the experience of contemporary adulthood involves at a fundamental level an interpretation of how new adults approach the indeterminacy of their futures. Central questions emerge: how can they establish a coherent biographical narrative in times of structural insecurities and a shifting value system that together posit the individual as increasingly self-responsible? To what extent are new adults' practices commensurate with contemporary social conditions? Do they defer or reject adulthood and remain, for an unspecifiable time, caught somewhere between adolescence and adulthood? Or do they in fact manage to be adults in their own right, and if so, how?

The respondents were initially chosen according to one criterion only: they had to be between the ages of 25 and 35 (the actual ages of respondents ranged from 25 to 32). I decided on this prerequisite for the simple reason that judging by the little consensus that does exist on "life stages" in the social sciences, and as reflected in national survey instruments such as the Australian Bureau of Statistics and the U.S. Census, persons up to the age of 24 (Australia) or 25 (U.S.) are generally considered nonadults, regardless what label is actually used to designate that status. Those who are 25 or older are generally considered adults, and that on the level of formal as well as informal cultural age norms. Adorno advised, "unless pre-scientific interests or extra-scientific concepts are imported into every scientific sociological investigation, then scientific interests and concepts are entirely lacking as well" (2000: 126). From this perspective, the fact that commonsense typifications attribute adult status to these individuals (even if discourse concerning young people "who refuse to grow up" delivers a different set of assumptions) is a relevant consideration. Furthermore, it is this age group (and increasingly beyond) that is the target of academic and popular discourse centering on the alleged postponement of adulthood. This is so because according to the normative view, these individuals should be grown up, that is, act and think in an adult manner as dictated by convention.

There is a class bias concerning the participants, although it is a bias that is contingent on their own positions rather than those of their parents. While half of them come from working-class backgrounds and the other half can be loosely categorized as middle-class, all but two studied at university at the time of the interviews. In terms of gender there is a slant toward men, with only four of the respondents being women. Both the class and gender aspects of the sample need to be qualified. The class bias can be defended on methodological grounds. For one, as I indicated in the introduction, this study is not intended to provide statistically verifiable, quantitative data and is therefore not bound by the requirement of a random sample. Second, by virtue of their educational qualifications, these individuals are supposed to have optimal life chances in Western, self-styled "knowledge societies." We cannot—and neither is it my intention to—accurately extrapolate from their experiences of adulthood the fates of those who live in poverty, are plagued by unemployment and underemployment, and suffer the social disrespect and indignities that come with marginality. But we can, I suggest, hazard an informed guess that an awareness of uncertainty, of the unknowability of the future, and a consequent lack of ability and/or desire to plan for the long term by those who are ostensibly best equipped to do so may also be reflected in perspectives of those who are in a less fortunate position. Note also that in the Australian context the equation university education = middle-class/relative affluence cannot be made in a straightforward manner. About 60 percent of all Australian students live below the poverty line, and the vast majority of students work part-time. A significant number of these work in two or three jobs (Sydney Morning Herald 2005). This does not take into account that some of these students receive support from their parents; but neither can we infer that all or even a majority do. Further, it is common practice among those Australian university students who leave the parental home to move into shared accommodation rather than reside in college dormitories, as is the case in the United States, for example.

This is an investigation of relatively recent (and sometimes only emergent) trends that are not equally present across society (even if we abstract from probable ethnic differences in perceptions and practices of adulthood). These trends are likely to be most salient in social strata where prolonged education and stay in the parental home, and geographical and professional mobility are the rule rather than the exception. In some ways the fact that the majority of the respondents were university students and thus assimilated a largely middle-class habitus facilitated the project: my questioning did not come as a surprise to them, the "restricted code" (Bernstein 1977) of the traditional working classes is outside their experience; the kinds of conversations we engaged in are as commonplace among them as the "ethics of authenticity" (Taylor 1991) are part of their practical consciousness. The above points pertain also to the gender question. There is, however, another issue here. While it would be unrealistic to speak of a complete leveling of opportunities that young women and men confront in Western societies, research has suggested that there is some conflation of gendered life experiences (Inglehart and Norris 2003). True, some of this leveling means men too are increasingly coming to experience the labor market insecurities that for a considerable period were the almost exclusive province of women.[1] On the positive side, there are good indications that interactions among young people are tending toward more democratic forms (Wilkinson and Mulgan 1995).

The Respondents

The respondents are assigned pseudonyms in order to ensure their anonymity. Here, then, is a brief introduction of the people who have so generously related their experiences. The details given below refer to the respondents' situations in 2002, the year throughout which the interviews took place.

Anthony (25) and *Greg* (26) both come from small country towns in New South Wales, the eastern state of which Sydney is the capitol. They moved to the metropolis some three years ago and work for a large retailer as shop assistants. This was where they met, subsequently to enter into an intimate relationship. They are cohabiting in a small apartment, which they share with two other people.

Christopher (25) was raised in the Blue Mountains to the west of Sydney. His parents both work in education. Christopher is undertaking studies in sociology and works part-time in a retail outlet. After breaking up with his girlfriend of several years, Christopher has just begun a new relationship. He lives in rental share accommodation with his partner and three other people.

David (29) grew up in a working-class suburb of Sydney. The first son of an ethnically mixed couple, he is the first member of his family to undertake tertiary studies. David has been in his current intimate relationship for two years. He lives at home with his parents and one of his two brothers.

Ethan (28) is a musician by trade and a former windsurfing champion. His sporting career was cut short by an accident and he subsequently decided to go back to university in order to further his education. Ethan grew up in suburban

Sydney, the only son of a working-class family. He is single and lives in rental share accommodation with four others.

Fred (26) is the son of Indian immigrants and was born in Australia. He is studying for a law degree and has several jobs. A former employee in a corporate bank, he works as a security guard by night, as the editor of a law journal, and as a junior advisor for a Member of Parliament, and does research work for an Australian film production company. He is single and lives with his parents.

Gavin (30) grew up in a single-parent middle-class household where he was raised by his mother, a sole parent. He was undertaking doctoral research in sociology until his partner's pregnancy. Gavin is the proud father of one-year-old twin girls and works part-time as a web designer and book reviewer. Unmarried, he lives in rental accommodation with his partner and children.

Henry (31) grew up on a small farm to the far west of Sydney. After having worked in odd jobs around the city for several years, Henry decided to study physiotherapy. He is single and lives in rental share accommodation.

Isabelle (30) is the daughter of an Irish-born mother, a senior nurse, and a Trinidadian father, a physician. Her parents divorced when she was 14. Isabelle was born in a large regional center north of Sydney and completed a liberal arts major in English some years ago. After having worked in various temporary jobs, Isabelle joined the public relations office of a reputable arts company. She has been with her partner for three years, and they both live in rental accommodation.

Karen (25) grew up in suburban Sydney, the daughter of South African immigrants who are employed in middle-managerial positions. She is studying economics, economic development, and Spanish. She is single, lives at home, and is about to embark on six months' study in Barcelona, Spain.

Louise (25) comes from a small New South Wales country town and is the daughter of a lawyer and a judge. She studies law part-time in Sydney and works as a casual employee in a retail outlet. She has been with her current partner for about three years and lives with him in rental accommodation.

Michelle (32) grew up in suburban Sydney in a working-class household and has lived away from home sporadically from age fifteen into her early twenties. She decided to go to university in 2000, where she studies for a liberal arts degree. Michelle makes her living as a professional belly dancer. After the recent breakdown of a long-term relationship she is newly single. She lives alone in rental accommodation.

What Does it Take to Be an Adult?

My first aim in conducting the interviews was to elicit respondents' perceptions about adulthood. "What does being adult, being grown up, mean?" was generally how I phrased this question. Another, related question had to do with the "how" and "when" of adulthood, that is, with memories of poignant events or moments that could be identified as a point of transition from adolescence to adulthood; its drift was: "Do you remember any events or moments that caused you to realize you had become an adult?" This question often triggered a more deliberate reflection on what was said in response to the first. Nearly always the answers began with a listing of the normative, objective markers of adulthood. For Gavin parenthood is the moment par excellence that ushers in that stage of life; Isabelle, in characteristically succinct fashion, mentions "getting a job, relationships, traveling"; for Henry it was moving from the country to the city at age eighteen; Ethan says it makes him think of "all the terrible clichés of suburban nuclear family madness," while Fred unwittingly elaborates what Ethan meant when he enumerates: "Work, family, all the conventional things, a house. You can't live with anybody else, so, being financially independent"—only to add, as certainties wane, "I don't know."

Predominantly, the respondents arrive at their individual interpretations of what adulthood involves by articulating what they think it is *not*. Thus, childhood constitutes the opposite of the images and narratives they provide in order to express what being grown up does and does not mean to them. Sometimes, as in Ethan's case, this is explicitly taken up: "I'm still defining it in relation to childhood. Maybe it has no meaning of itself." Sometimes they slip back into their childhood shoes and revive or construct earlier sentiments about adults, as Ethan does at another point: "It's taken me a long time to get through a received notion that I had as a child, that adults are somehow complete, that you start to be an adult and then you are a complete person." These insights are expressions of a deep-seated cultural association: that adulthood equals full personhood, that coming of age means to make the journey from "human becoming" to "human being." But at the same time there is recognition that what is posited as a goal eludes definition; it is an insight that gets to the core of my investigation: "Childhood has so many milestones. Like, every birthday is defining. Adulthood sort of ends up being a big mish-mash" (Louise).

This juxtaposing of childhood and adulthood in order for one to come into relief against the other is not particularly remarkable. After all, we are aware from a young age that we will become grown-ups one day. That process calls for one stage of life to be left behind and another to be entered, and so our perceptions of one are dependent on the other. It allows us to imagine the next stage in the previous one. The notion of a transition from childhood to adulthood is thus quasi-natural. Moreover, my question concerning poignant moments of transition perhaps sensitized the respondents to that very fact. But what *is* remarkable is that, for all their differences, all interviewees without exception at some point during the conversation came to realize that something was unclear. Thinking about a commonsensical notion shattered the familiar; their confidence in what adulthood meant diminished as they began to question and tried to articulate a notion they had rarely reflected upon before. Reflection also meant that usually the discussion shifted to a less straightforward terrain to include general themes such as maturity, social competencies, economic and political uncertainty, and generational differences. But not only did the answers tend to become more nuanced; due to the more individually targeted quality of the question concerning transitionary events, the respondents tended to focus on subjective matters. In fact, they overwhelmingly posited adulthood in terms of subjective changes and developments. Karen's response is for all its brevity an eloquent and paradigmatic statement of a general sentiment about adulthood echoed in various ways by most participants: "It's a state of mind."

An increasing self-confidence and assuredness, self-discipline and control over the emotions, responsible and principled action, tolerance for, or acceptance of, difference, and the freedom from peer pressure that comes with increased self-knowledge are some of the details these young adults sketch against the conceptual background of adulthood as a state of mind. These subjective processes of personal development toward psychological maturity are rarely linked to aspirations toward the more traditional, objective/social connotations of adulthood. Indeed, Fred by first impulse connects one objective marker—parenthood—with the most salient *attitude* it requires in his view: "You . . . have to subordinate your desires to the desires of . . . your dependents." That is, the *objective* achievements so indicative of standard adulthood are only considered insofar as a link to their *subjective relevance* can be established. Hence, even the social recognition attained for one's generativity is plumbed for psychological returns.

The respondents see the transition to adulthood as a "state of mind" as contingent upon experiences that lead to a self-revaluation of some kind. By extension, "there is," as Karen puts it, "no clear definition as to where it [adulthood] begins and where it ends." As the normative model of adulthood nears its demise in practice, it is relegated to the realm of ideas; the objective, collectively understood transitions into adulthood give way to less definable, subjective events. To the same measure, the onset and duration of adulthood become blurred. The "liminality without limits" (chapter 4) so indicative of the new adulthood finds expression in these young people's experiences.

Some respondents explicitly attend to this characteristic aspect of the new adulthood. Asked about transitionary moments, Ethan refers to (plural) "critical moments, critical situations, important relationships that precipitate certain changes in one's concept of one's self." Likewise, David speaks of "heaps of moments," and points out that "with each successive moment you think you have come of age again." But, to make matters more complicated still, there is no guarantee that such moments provide certainty: "What I might have perceived as growth," David muses, "might have actually been some kind of regression." The very opacity that comes with the conceptualization of adulthood in terms of self-perception also means that there is, in principle, no reason why the insight that one is grown up should remain eternally valid; by extension, it is potentially forever subject to revision.

While some of the interviewees equate transitionary events to independence, most refer to a sense of personal growth expressed in various ways—some similar, some contradictory—but almost always with characteristic vagueness. Independence comes in many forms. Louise, for instance, not without a sense of the banality of these episodes, recalls her delight at "buying sweets in the supermarket and eating them on the way home before the evening meal and not having someone tell you "'don't do that before dinner.'" The very triviality of this example is evidence for the depth of the cultural value of autonomy.

Anthony picks up the thread of consumption when he mentions "buying the things you want" as the key gain that comes with financial independence. Others mention traveling without their parents, the end of an intimate relationship rather than their first sexual experience (something that for most occurred too early to be associated with entry into adulthood, thus exemplifying the rift between physiological and social maturation), obtaining their driver's license, getting their first job, or moving out of home into share accommodation. These events and experiences are naturally assumed to be personal business, and personal business only. This perspective posits the transition to adulthood, however partial or incomplete, as a subjective phenomenon. From this view, adulthood indeed appears to be above all a psychological category and thus the respondents' views seem to confirm extant research. What this proposition ignores, however, is the social constructedness of those transitionary events—the culturally framed repertoire, selection from which assures the proper association between the transitionary moment in question and adulthood as a social category. Seen in this way, the social core of adulthood remains salient, individuals' psychological conceptualizations notwithstanding. But due to the conceptual fragility of the mostly ad hoc, subjectively conceived transitions, for the respondents the social basis of adulthood—adult recognition—lies obscured from view.

Many respondents attempt to express what this development has meant for them. There is Michelle, who simply states: "I know better what I want and what I don't want"; or Anthony and Greg, who agree that "you have more confidence in yourself"; or Karen, who phrases it as "an acceptance of me." But there are also those who delve deeper and try to interpret their memories in order to express what it was that triggered their perceived growth in the first place. These accounts merit closer attention.

Independence and Power

Common sense and research have it that growing up has something to do with gaining independence in its various forms. Material as well as psychological independence, having to take responsibility for your own life, and sometimes for the lives of dependents, is the usual way in which an achieved, separate adult identity is framed. But rarely do commentators connect independence with its less salutary flip side: a sense of isolation that sometimes comes as the price for a newly realized freedom. It was therefore surprising that this should have developed into a thematic thread plotted by more than one of the respondents: "I guess [there were] moments when I have sensed my own isolation, when as a child I would have asked for help and expect[ed] to receive it, moments when I . . . might have called for help and not received it because people . . . thought, "'He is an adult, he needs to work it out.'" Or when I've just hesitated and gone, "'you just have to deal with it by yourself'" (Ethan). Fred also identified a sense of aloneness, one that is strongly connected to another realization, namely, that not everybody "has your best interests at heart": "There comes a certain point where you find that people are in fact acting against your interest, or they won't give you a break if you stuff up. They will say, "'well, too bad'" . . . and you realize, "'Oh my God, no one is gonna look after me. I have to look after myself; I'm completely an independent and discrete person.'" Christopher too connects the "feeling of independence" to new uncertainties that arise when we gain freedom from the "people and institutions that you had reliance on and had a security within." So, there is a sense that as adults individuals have to tackle the world on their own, develop competencies such as self-reliance, and take responsibility for their actions within much smaller margins for error. As David puts it: "You are thrown out into the world, and I think that's when you feel like "'Hey, I have to start becoming an adult, take my own responsibilities . . . [make] my own fate as opposed to relying on others.'" But self-reliance brings with it something else: having to deal with people outside the private sphere of the family on your own terms as a unique social being. That sense of individuation is sometimes accompanied by the realization that power and politics, and appearances rather than substance, are intrinsic to the world of adults.

I am reminded here of a passage in Michel Houellebecq's novel *Atomised* (2001), where a young girl, Annabelle, comes to a similar understanding. She arrives home after having been kissed by a friend who, according to all the advice she had received in a teen magazine, was never supposed to cross that line, who should have remained a platonic "best friend":

> It was barely eleven o'clock when she arrived, and there was a light on in the living room. When she saw the light, she started to cry. It was here, on a July night in 1974, that Annabelle accepted the painful but unequivocal truth that she was an individual. An animal's sense of self emerges through physical pain, but individuality in human society only attains true self-consciousness by the intermediary of mendacity, with which it is sometimes confused. At the age of 16, Annabelle had kept no secrets from her parents, nor had she—and she now realized that this was a rare and precious thing—from Michel [her actual boyfriend]. In a few short hours that evening, Annabelle had come to realize that life was

an unrelenting succession of lies. It was then, too, that she became aware of her beauty. (2001: 89)

Firstly, there is the realization of dishonesty as a part of life—part of what we understand by "loss of innocence"—that accompanies growing up. And secondly, her experience means that Annabelle now knows that she has fallen (and will continue to fall) victim to her appeal, but at the same time be able to take advantage of it for her own ends. Appearance serves as protection from the mendacity of the adult world by allowing individuals to be part of a world not just as passive objects, as the perceived case was during childhood and adolescence, but also as active and self-aware actors. Fred's thoughts evoke similar insights. Dishonesty and appearances are two motifs he reiterates and elaborates in his remarks. His statements warrant an interpretation of some length.

Presentation of Self and Individuation

For Fred, growing up has to do with participation in power struggles of a particular kind: personal politics; and it was upon entering work that this became most immediately apparent to him:

> It's very competitive and it's quite political . . . it's office politics. Everyone presents the façade of friendliness. If you are still in the mode of being a kid you're trusting everybody and you think, "everybody is nice, and everybody has my best interests at heart" . . . and you are quite rudely shocked to find out that it's a whole world of appearances and tact; people pursuing interests through politics, personal politics, which is very different from when you're a child of course. Your parents look out for you, and your friends are too inexperienced to use too much tact, or too much politics. . . . When you start having contact with the grown up world you get confronted with these things, you start feeling the pressure that, "oh no, I have to start engaging in this, I have to look after my own interests otherwise I'm gonna be harmed." That's one of the moments when I said, "ok, I have to start becoming an adult."

According to Fred, adult personal politics is qualitatively different from the squabbles and differences he might have had with peers at an earlier age. For adults it is imperative to be able to draw upon personal skills in order to deal with different viewpoints and opinions, with others' competitiveness and sometimes malice, in a tactful, more restrained manner. This requires young adults to become more circumspect about people, more discriminating about whom to trust and when. And crucially, for Fred this means that we need to be able to *act* in an adult manner, to enter the "world of appearances and tact," as he puts it, when this is deemed apposite. In fact, Fred reinforces what researchers claim: that knowing when what type of behavior is appropriate or inappropriate, and that mastering a variety of conventions in a variety of contexts are central social competencies of adulthood (e.g., Smart and Sanson 2003). How we negotiate these aspects of life, how well we are able to maintain and sustain the "façade" of adulthood, as Fred calls it, codetermines the degree of adult recognition we are granted. The dramaturgical presentation of an adult self, to appropriate Goffman (1959), is vital, indeed normative, as it comes with sanctions attached. Fred remarks: "There are certain mores . . . a common mode of interaction that you need to present to be an adult. . . . And when you deviate away from that . . . [this] contributes to your [perceived] incompetence . . . because you can't present yourself as an adult in that way."

Learning the conventions of adult social intercourse is vital to coming of age. What gives it particular significance in the contemporary era is that this no longer occurs in concert with the attainment of objective social markers. Rather, the subjective mastery of "the arts of impression management" (Goffman 1959) takes precedence over the substantive realization of traditional signifiers. For Fred the struggle for recognition requires the ability to mold himself to the interaction requirements of social settings other than the family. This by no means excludes acting "like a child" when it is socially called for:

> I often present myself to other people not as an adult. Even though I can present myself as an adult, I don't. Just because I find that . . . especially in my jobs or places where I work I often come in contact with people much older than myself . . . so, obviously if I do present myself as an adult they usually have problems with that because they consider me to be precocious and they get quite annoyed that I'd done more than them. . . . So I present myself often as a kid or someone who needs instruction . . . even though I don't really need it, just for that situation.

Here Fred reiterates the cultural association of adulthood with competence and full personhood. Also, for Fred, age norms do not enter the equation. It is as if performing certain roles negates the distinctions between adolescents and adults based on our perceptions of age. Adulthood is here overwhelmingly framed in terms of competencies the acquisition of which allows effective participation in and integration into public milieus.

Sometimes it is a particularly dramatic episode that lets people see through the veil of adult infallibility. David came to the aid of his father who, in a fit of rage, staged a mock suicide attempt, as it turned out: "I realized that he was holding onto the rope and that this was all a façade and beyond that, he was pretending that he had died as well." That loss of faith in the parent's integrity caused the son to realize that the words and actions of those closest to him were not to be totally relied upon (however fortunate the outcome was in this case). It also meant that from that point on it became increasingly important to David to be more honest, to have "principles" and to be "able to stay true to them." This was a significant transition to what David perceives to be an ideal adulthood—though it is a transition that is entirely self-referential. The transition to adulthood conceived as a journey into the world of appearances also means to leave behind an idealized childhood and adolescence where, unperturbed by social norms, authentic expression is still something unselfconscious individuals engage in and expect of others. By contrast, in Fred's perception adulthood is the time of instrumental action where a "skill set" enables us to become effective participants in a society that values surface presentations over content. Central to the acquisition of such skills, to "do the things that grown-ups do," are "self-discipline and control over our emotions." Though Fred affirms that this is "not necessarily instrumentally" conceived—control and discipline are, for him, prerequisites "for your own freedom to do things"—he concedes in the same breath that this "helps you achieve more things." So, although he expresses the intention to marshal his social competencies for substantive matters, Fred accords primacy to the instrumental benefits of self-control and discipline in the adult world.

According to some of the respondents, adulthood, whichever form it may take and however many events will resemble its attainment, requires us to unlearn an unselfconscious way of life and to acquire a strategic attitude. Above all, it is about "learning the modes of interaction which everyone knows to be adult, to signify you as an adult . . . and, secondly, to learn to do this competently." Fred also alludes here to the fact that adult behavior consists of shared cultural norms. That is, the subjective competencies he refers to are not competencies he has independently attributed to adulthood, but constitute components of an extant normative frame of reference; there are, as he says, "modes of interaction . . . everyone knows to be adult," and in so doing he hints at modes of adult recognition.

The social conventions of adulthood go hand in hand with a more material dimension: "You need to have certain stuff to be an adult. For example, you need to have a car or some kind of mode of transport to be an adult, I think. If you're taking public transport . . . I don't think you can be as adult as if you have a car and you can say, "'Yeah I drive there,'" or "'I pick you up.'" The clothes you wear as well are very important. I think when you start shopping at, say, David Jones [a department store that presents itself as relatively upmarket] for your casual clothes I know that you definitely know you are a grown-up. . . . Of course, other people seeing you as an adult is very important." Here, Fred again expresses a clear awareness that adulthood is contingent on the granting of respect by others, something that, again, relies heavily on surface appearances. His idea of adult recognition, however, reflects a premodern attribution of status along the lines of prestige or honor; it is a stratified view, which implies that adulthood is a matter of class; but it also indicates to what extent the valorization of money influences individuals' notions of personhood in contemporary society. Fred reiterates this later when he says, "When other people see you as an adult . . . you join in a kind of society of adults." According to Fred, then, social esteem can partly be procured in the market. To the extent that this is so, adulthood hinges on its affordability. Moreover, the price of adulthood changes according to class position: "For instance some people I work with at parliament. Or, say, lawyers I know. . . . For them you can't be respected . . . if you don't have a house or a car or certain stuff. Because if they say, "look I'm having a party this weekend, come over to my place" and you go, "oh, is there a train station close by" [laughs] that's quite embarrassing."

In sum, for Fred adulthood is about clearly mapping life according to means/ends calculations, something that confounds the reputed postmaterialism of his generation. "You have to become goal orientated I suppose," as he puts it. This calls for a change in value orientation: the perceived naïveté and innocent trust of childhood are exchanged for the circumspection—and even distrust—of adulthood. And so entering the world of adults, reliant as this process is on recognition by others, means to engage in the drama of personal politics, but also in the comedy of instrumental adult self-presentation, in order to gain the respect of others; in order to further your occupational opportunities; and, finally, in order to gain a measure of self-respect.

By drawing on Goffman, we can further emphasize the point that Fred's performance of adulthood is not just a one-way street; it indicates that social recognition is intersubjectively constituted because it is not just about his fitting into existing social environments, but also about making demands on others so that recognition of his full adult status can be obtained: "[W]hen an individual projects a definition of the situation and thereby makes an implicit or explicit claim to be a person of a particular kind, he automatically exerts a moral demand upon the others, obliging them to value and treat him in the manner that persons of his kind have a right to expect" (Goffman 1959: 13). For Fred it is in the arena of work, and more specifically the professional environs of a big corporation, that this performance is to be sustained. Failure to do so would cause colleagues to lose respect for him; colleagues who themselves are, perhaps to varying degrees of awareness, knowing participants in the play of adulthood. This mode of adulthood is seemingly divorced from a constructed self, which in the process of growing up sets out to attain for itself the trappings of what being grown up is about—while the *real* self, conceived as an essential core that has simply always been there, looks on, evaluates, and makes the necessary adjustments. In this process of self-monitoring and self-assessment Fred deploys psychological competencies like self-discipline and self-control, marshals the personal skills of tact and impression management, and engages in specific consumption patterns in order to assuage the threat of disrespect. But there is a contradiction here: because for Fred adulthood is what childhood is not, this fear of not being taken seriously also suggests a fear of an involuntary relapse to an earlier phase of life. The dispositions equated with that phase of life are performed only when forms of adult sociability demand it. Yet, at the same time there is a sense of nostalgia at having left behind a more unadulterated way of being that was closer to who Fred feels he "really" is. That contradiction is most apparently resolved by the ability to choose adulthood (non-childhood) as a performed act in a particular sphere, most notably the sphere of work. This indicates that being grown up does not have to be settled once and for all; it is a way of being that can be drawn upon according to situations and circumstances.

The fear of relapse into non-adulthood is the fear of a loss of personhood. But that loss seems to be of greatest consequence when a career is at stake. Here too, it seems, the prevalent dynamics of recognition are not fixed. A measure of social competence is required that allows individuals to project *degrees* of personhood according to given demands, such as existing hierarchical inequalities. This does not mean, however, that one's adulthood—one's full personhood—is compromised. The awareness of socially constituted asymmetries and their appropriate negotiation is an important aspect of social competence, the successful deployment of which contributes to individuals' adult recognition.

Particularly in the conversation with Fred, but to some extent also in my dialogues with Ethan, David, and Christopher, the theme of authenticity is strongly present. As we have seen, they perceive adulthood as that phase or stage of life whose entry requires individuals to let go of an authentic life already led during the more innocent years of childhood and adolescence. This perception reverses the notion that individuation occurs in the course from adolescence to adulthood. In fact, Fred and Ethan in particular hint at a kind of deindividuation as part of growing up; and in so doing they turn the Jungian conception of individuation against itself and also unwittingly challenge Eriksonian notions of adolescent identity-formation: "You have to learn to be untrusting of others. . . . You have to learn to *alienate yourself* from your emotions, objectify, control, learn tact, present yourself in a certain way, *lack complete integrity* to who you are . . . that's what you have to learn to become an adult" (Fred). The world of adults, as perceived by Fred, is the world of appearances, a world that privileges form over content. These sentiments are echoed by Ethan, who talks about "this façade of perfection, or this façade of infallibility that a lot of adults have." And although the respondents intimate that, in Jungian fashion, they perceive individuation as a process that takes place *against* external social constraint rather than as a consequence of a creative/productive relationship between the demands of various social milieus and self-assertion, for them this augurs a loss—not a gain—of integrity. The internalization of social conventions is seen as a hindrance to authentic being. Social competencies such as tact and civility—seen by some as necessary ingredients of public interaction (e.g., Sennett 1992)—are viewed as little more than obligatory concessions to a charade of sociability. The acting out of pre-adult impulses would most likely be counterproductive if by social competence we understand, as a minimal definition, "socially acceptable, learned ways of behaving that enable a person to interact effectively with other people" (Gresham and Elliot quoted in Smart and Sanson 2003: 4). But the fact that Fred schematized these issues with specific reference to work suggests that adulthood as full personhood is indeed subject to variable, milieu-specific relations of adult recognition.

Just as for many respondents growing up has to do with recognizing and then learning to tactfully adjust to the social norms of adulthood, so Christopher too speaks of a "loss of innocence" that comes with attaining "a perspective [that says] that the world's not as it seems." He connects this with the insight that social sensibility at times requires the subordination of his own standpoint to that of others, regardless of whether he agrees or not: "I might think it's crap what [people] are saying, but you have to negotiate that difference rather than [insist on your own view]." For Christopher this has less to do with playing the game of personal politics, but rather with acquiring a more externally directed perspective: "I guess I'm thinking of the way you treat people, and particularly in work situations and in intimate situations; that it's coming to acknowledge that you're bound to have a different worldview to the people that you're interacting with, rather than thinking you know how it is or thinking others are wrong." And like Fred, Christopher refers to "malice," though in a qualitatively different sense. For him, the possibility of antagonism is an existential constant regardless of age. What has changed in the process of his growing up is Christopher's stance toward people who act in malevolent ways, that is, the way he contextualizes the motives for their actions and attitudes: "I was so reluctant to accept that people do act maliciously. And I used to justify that out by looking at their circumstances, looking at their set of experiences, but then I guess this is a huge thing of adulthood for me, and where I've changed in the way I see people: there has to be a point where someone has to take responsibility for their actions."

Christopher concedes that there are more sanguine aspects to growing up. These have to do with a balanced view of self and others, expressed in two motifs. One is about balancing the assumption that people's circumstances determine their behavior with the demand that they—at a point—take responsibility for their actions. Secondly, growing up is also about replacing an earlier egocentrism with a more pluralist understanding of difference. Ethan contributes a related insight: "Maybe part of adulthood is a capacity to be more open to the world, which is something we normally ascribe to children." At the heart of this process of moral conversion lies another psychological prerequisite, one that is firmly anchored in the cultural idea of maturity:

> I think for me, personally, it's a consolidation of a sense of self-assuredness and confidence which makes it [adulthood] seem different to youth. I'm not as vulnerable to the whims of others or the ways I perceive I should respond in a situation. I guess it's more of an arrogance that says, "'This is how I'm gonna respond in this situation,'" rather than feeling coerced into responding in a certain way . . . I think the way, as a kid, I can remember having treated people sometimes . . . which I think stems from that sense of threat and vulnerability. I simply don't feel the need [to do that] anymore. So confrontation for me has changed, and the nature of confrontation. (Christopher)

Both Fred and Christopher acknowledge the differences between the worlds of adolescents and adults in similar ways. They confirm that entering the normative bounds of adulthood means having to modify your behaviors and attitudes, and they both conceive of this as a loss of naïveté. But they differ in their judgments concerning the ultimate ends of this self-development. While Fred is ambivalent, swaying between acknowledging the merits of self-discipline, and regretting having to enter and play along with the histrionics of adult sociability, Christopher sees in the very difference of others' perspectives, and in the ever-present possibility of negotiation, an opportunity for personal growth. "This kind of a loss of innocence is OK," he says.

Although the psychological aspects of adulthood are in themselves hardly new—the nineteenth-century *Bildungsroman* being a case in point—there is a qualitative difference in the present context: adulthood as a state of mind is a consequence of new adults' self-reflexivity, which, in turn, seems to allow for a calibrated, instrumental deployment of adult competencies as required at given occasions. But more importantly, it is perhaps simply the case that adulthood's psychological components appear more salient, take on heightened significance, precisely because the objective criteria of old are losing empirical validity. How this loss of determinacy is dealt with is the subject of the next chapter.

6

New Adult Voices II:
Without a Center that Holds

"Wish fulfillment is the death of future."

Christopher

Having expressed what adulthood means to them, how they perceive the dynamics of independence and power and the modes of self-presentation these at times require, the new adults at the center of this study dug deeper still to ponder their place in the world and how they cope with uncertainty. In so doing they provide us with some insights into the subjective and shared repertoire on which they draw in the creation of a new adulthood.

Two Adulthoods

The respondents' views show that they are highly aware of belonging to a generation whose historical situation is markedly discontinuous with their parents' generation above and beyond the minutiae of individual biographies. Their considerations, in total, signify an awareness of a collective fate and thus of generational identification.

Several of the interviewees identified early marriage and family formation as something that was common for the previous generation. In addition, they were keenly aware that the decision to marry early and have children young did not just rest on individual desires isolated from social pressures, but was connected to strongly normative cultural values: "Without a doubt they [the parents] are probably a good ten years ahead in terms of when they got their mortgage, or settled down, or whatever. I mean, they were too young in my opinion. My mum was probably about 20 when she had my first brother. I mean I can't imagine that. And she used to say to me: "'That's your problem. When I was your age I had three kids.'" But I think it was expected of them more so [than now]. There was more pressure on; it was the done thing, as a rule" (Michelle). Fred echoes these sentiments:

> They have a very set progression from . . . childhood to adulthood and they say that they grew up much earlier than I did. They went to school, then to university, they got married when they were 24, and they had me when they were 25. They say, "Adulthood was thrust upon us, because we had you. We had to support a child, we had to get a house, we had to do all that stuff, set up business. We weren't completely ready for it, but we had to grow up and we had to take on the responsibilities of adulthood, and we had to get on with it." So that's obviously different. . . . This is what everyone was doing at the time.

Anthony, commenting on the changed nature of family formation in his generation, insists, "These days when you grow up you are not growing up to get married and pregnant, just spitting out children. That's what they [the previous generation] did." Implying a transformation of social norms, Greg adds: "They don't push you to do these things any more." Today's young adults are aware that their growing up is drastically different from that of their parents' generation. There is also a sense that this difference is based partly on the demise of social pressures to conform to the normative model of adulthood (in some social groups at least). With this they tacitly attribute the social markers of marriage and family formation to the adulthood of another generation.

For some interviewees the possibilities for long-term life planning in the past, and their relative lack in the present, are fundamental in their comparisons between their parents' growing up and their own. Christopher makes the point strongly: "I think it's a huge, huge difference that my parents and most people of that generation could assume they were gonna get a job, and could assume that they could get a fulltime job. And so there follows a whole lot of presumptions from that: "'I'll probably be able to buy a house, I'll probably be able to buy a car,'" these material things. But also, it's not as much of a preoccupation in a sense." To emphasize the then-unquestioned normality of this situation, he adds that this was so for his parents even though they were following a usual path: "And I find it strange because my parents were unorthodox in the sense that they actively and consciously tried to break that mold." Christopher's perplexity can be demystified: precisely because the normative model of adulthood represented an overarching frame of reference, it provided a bedrock of security that existed in principle for everyone, even for those who did not fit into that frame; even for those who did not envisage themselves as having to rely on those securities. Those who "broke the mold" still knew *what* mold they were breaking, *what* they were gaining or losing, embracing or rejecting, in *what* social context. Importantly, Christopher also points out that the very fact that life could be planned when long-term, fulltime employment was a distinct possibility for most meant that planning hardly needed to preoccupy people. Not so for his generation: "You can't expect . . . the flow of things, like it's going to be normal. And I do expect, you know, I'll probably have four different careers. That would have never crossed my parents' generation's mind."

Some respondents allude to historical contingencies in trying to explain the changes that have occurred. Ethan, for instance, speaks of a need for security that arose directly from the lived-through trauma of earlier generations: "Many of my parents' generation seemed to have lived under a couple of big clouds. One was the Great Depression. My father was born in 1934, and my mother is a bit younger than that. They grew up through an economy of scarcity and a fear that whatever you've got might be taken away from you real soon. . . . In terms of a yearning for some sort of security or to buffer themselves against those insecurities . . . that stuff sort of still looms." That desire for security, the possibility for its realization after the Second World War, and the value orientation of conformity, make for a constellation of historical, structural, and cultural factors with which the normative model of adulthood has strong affinities.

While the respondents point to the relative ease with which the previous generation could map out their adult lives, they also think that their own opportunities to self-fashion their biographies are incomparably greater. What is more, there is a general consensus that the uncertainty of the present is preferable to the security without opportunity of the past. To illustrate, let us return to Christopher's thoughts on intergenerational differences: "I think uncertainty has become a taken-for-granted part of my life, in a way that it wasn't for them, and I think . . . it's a normal state of affairs [for us] whereas I just don't think my parents' generation would conceptualize it in the same way." As a consequence of this normalization of uncertainty it is not necessarily perceived in negative terms. To the contrary, behind thinly veiled objective precariousness lies the ever-present potential of more freedom: "I think this is where I see a transformative potential and hope. When contingency and uncertainty are normals of existence, your receptivity to change is higher, because change becomes a more normal aspect of life."

There are statements by others that resonate with this attitude. "I'm open to change, I don't have a certain plan, and I'm alright with that," says Karen, and compares this perspective to that of an older generation that she perceives as "closed to change." As we recall from chapter 2, underlying the perception of adaptability to change, and thus individuals' ability to counter any untoward consequences that may arise, is a strong belief in the existence of options in all spheres of life and a trust that, confronted with these, they will make the right choices. Again, the previous generation serves as the foil against which present options and opportunities are projected and evaluated: "There are that many more opportunities at your fingertips these days. . . . Our lives are much more diverse, there is more choice" (Greg). "The choices that we have; like career choices, especially for women; the opportunity to live overseas; the opportunity to have careers. There is a lot more opportunity, a lot more choice for people in my generation than in my parents'" (Isabelle). "There is too much to experience now, the world is so much more open . . . there's so many opportunities. I can work overseas; I can do anything" (Henry). And in a more qualified fashion: "However limited in practice the range of choices actually is . . . I think it is a bigger component" (Christopher). These statements make it clear that the material security and predictability of their parents' lives hold, for these people, little to be desired. Living with risk is as normal for them as the uncertainty it engenders; after all, such is the world into which this generation was born. Yet, the acceptance of uncertainty as a way of life and the identification of personal development as the major indicator of adulthood do not necessarily imply that they are fully grown up. Because however alien notions of long-term employment, family, marriage, and independent living are for most of them, in the final analysis it is precisely these objective markers and social badges of adulthood that are most overtly connected with being grown up.

But at the same time, these young adults also feel uneasy about some of the attitudinal aspects they attribute to *that* adulthood; and invariably they see that kind of adulthood as belonging to another generation. As Ethan remarks: "Adulthood seems like the full-stop I'm reluctant to apply." Likewise, Michelle says, "I guess I see that whole adult thing as not my style. I don't think you can define yourself as one hundred percent adult. That for me has implications of being serious and uptight, boring." And Christopher finds the notion of reaching destination adulthood inconceivable: "We are told it's a process with an endpoint that you arrive at, but I can't imagine how I'll ever arrive at that endpoint." There is, then, a distinct sense that these young people live two adulthoods: one that is authentic and "in here," and one that is inauthentic and "out there." After all, they do know that they are adults, but not quite in the way that this is expected of them, although playing along with the normative model is sometimes necessary. However, they do this when required not so much for the self, but in order to make a place for themselves in the world "out there." Theirs is a new adulthood, which they are defining for themselves against and within the normative constraints of standard adulthood. That is to say, they assert their own adulthood *against* the other insofar as their practices and orientations conflict with that ideal; and they forge their new adulthood *within* the other insofar as the latter still constitutes a part of the world in which they have to live, a world in the redefinition of which they are most actively engaged.

Two sets of values sit side by side here. On the one hand the respondents value personal development toward maturity; in fact many of them insist that they have achieved a good measure of responsibility, have decided on moral principles, and have gained cognitive independence and confidence so that *psychologically* they perceive themselves as complete. But on the other hand they eschew the material and social markers of standard adulthood that connote "settling down" and the mentality their actualization presumably requires. As I have discussed in previous chapters, settling down in the classic sense is today for a variety of social reasons much more difficult than in the past. In addition, this is bolstered by the subjective realization that even though a protracted period of open-ended choices and decisions brings with it difficulties, it is also attractive—more attractive, it seems, than the finality standard adulthood appears to promise. This, I suggest, is intimately connected to these young adults' estimation of the future, a future they perceive as "pregnant with potential" (Christopher) as it appears empty of concrete content.

A New Fatalism

Decidedly the most prevalent attitude regarding the respondents' life trajectories is a proclivity toward *keeping the future open*, meaning that the indeterminate period of time yet to be experienced is best kept free of planned goals. Rather than a progression through a series of stations, they perceive this development as a flow without predetermined checkpoints or definite direction. Christopher puts it succinctly: "I really see my own future as an open book." Ethan expresses a similar opinion in a more indirect fashion: "Time is more flexible for me than ever before. If I have an hour left or a hundred years, it doesn't have to make too much difference." Some also suggest that a noncommittal or ambiguous attitude regarding their futures is not just an individually chosen way to look at life. They imply that this is simply how the world is, although why this may be so remains largely unarticulated. They want to keep open a future that is open; a future that allows for little self-projection: "I think it's [the future] very contingent. . . . I have no idea what I'm gonna be doing in a couple of years. I'm just gonna have to see what happens and then make a decision as it comes . . . and that's work. But in . . . personal life as well, I mean you don't know what the hell is gonna happen, I mean how do you know? Everything is so contingent" (Fred). Or as Henry puts it: "You can't really plan your future, not even in a specialized job . . . I hardly ever plan more than six months to a year ahead. You have ideas as to what you wanna do, but, I mean, so many times they have fallen through . . . I suppose you can plan, but you can't expect what's gonna happen." What is expressed here is not just the realization that a future time is suffused with contingency, but also that this very realization stems from the respondents' experiences of an ever-changing present: "You can plan. But it never works out. I've even found that in the last couple of years. I'd just say, "'in six months I'll do that'" and something else happens. Six months ago I was living in Kingsford, no, Kensington. See? I don't even know [laughs]. I thought, "'yeah, maybe I do the editor thing'"; and six months later I'm working for this state minister. It's just crazy" (Fred). Planning is doubly prejudiced: there is fear of planning, for it holds within it the possibility of closure, of finitude. At the same time, planning is impossible due to the continuous changes, the fluidity of the present.

This stands in stark contrast to the experiences of the parent generation. While the parents were able to rely on the long term as a relatively predictable continuum along which mortgages and children were calculable projects, and work was much easier to obtain and retain, for this generation the long term is no longer a valid precept. I have referred to this in chapter 2 as the generational shift from the *unnecessary possibility, to the impossible necessity* of planning. This was a salient generational difference articulated by these young adults. How this difference is interpreted and then translated into a stance toward the future is plain in Karen's thoughts: "I'm not the kind of person that sets like a ten-year plan that has to be met. . . . I think that's a characteristic of a lot of people my age, who are just open to change and open to opportunity. Whereas the older generation *need* that set plan, they *need* an idea of how they gonna go from one place to the next." This is a case of misinterpretation that arises from contemporary modernity's epistemological fallacy, that is, people's diminishing ability to connect their own destinies with the social forces that shape them. Thus, Karen attributes systemic factors to individuals' mentalities. While the possibility to plan meant that this was, in fact, not of great urgency for the previous generation, in her mind this is evidence of individuals' need to plan; and the current impossibility to plan is expressed in the language of individual freedom. In fact, the knowledge that the future is contingent engenders optimism in most, as they equate the unpredictability of their life trajectories with an abundance of opportunity. Michelle's statement is a prime example: "I'm completely unsure; it's all a bit blank, but I'm excited." And Greg mentions that although he does not have "any grand plans," he too is "quite optimistic about the future," while Karen also professes her excitement: "It's exciting . . . there is so much to discover . . . there is so much out there." "[The future is] contingent, pregnant with potential," as Christopher puts it, while Henry remarks: "I mean it's good to have goals, but I believe it's also good to have your options open . . . you might be so focused on something that you may have not experienced other things and as you experience those more you might be more inclined towards them."

While the respondents perceive the future as uncertain, as open, this indeterminacy has its salutary side. Temporal openness is key to the promises of things to come. Henry, like others, intimates that the future is to be kept open and that in that very openness lies the possibility for advancement, achievement, and fulfillment. This exemplifies an attitudinal element that helps to connect two aspects of the new adulthood I have pointed out above: the awareness of uncertainty that comes with the recognition that the future is now more unknowable than was the case for previous generations, and the related feeling that a long-range mapping of concrete life goals is impossible and even undesirable. It is implicit in these views that the absence of concrete goals is ameliorated by a more flexible attitude: to make the most of life, to make the best possible deal. Thus, "it's all good" a throwaway line for all situations has for good reasons become the fatalistic mantra of a generation (R. Mead 2001). Rather than uncertainty being countered with a plan-at-all-costs attitude, the future is not only recognized as indeterminate, but also actively constructed as such.

As I suggested in chapter 2, however paradoxical this may seem at first glance, the construction of an open future is intimately related to an anthropological constant: individuals' need for control over their lives. The key to resolving this paradox lies in linking interviewees' perceptions about opportunities, options, and uncertainties to an aspect that is fundamental to the open-ended characteristic of capitalist societies: the in-principle infinity of possibilities and options. This taken-for-granted assumption enables people to indefinitely delay ultimate, once-and-for-all choices. In an epigrammatic statement, Christopher expresses the motivating sentiment: "Wish fulfillment is the death of future." It is not just that the future is incalculable, planning nonsensical, and therefore life ever more contingent; on the contrary, keeping the future open is precisely the means by which these new adults deal with uncertainty. This future-openness cum present-centeredness is a rational response to a world that is inherently unstable, unpredictable, and contingent: "The best thing is not to make these plans and do things as they come. . . . There is more uncertainty now, and I guess that's one way for us to deal with that uncertainty. I mean it's a very romantic way of dealing with it as well . . . but it's realistic because you can't plan anything any more" (Karen).

These are signs of a new fatalism that are evident in statements such as "[doing] things as they come," or "I guess it's that idea of floating, which in some ways I'm kind of attracted to" (Christopher), and, "I think sometimes I'm a bit blasé about the future as well . . . whatever happens will happen" (David). However, this mentality differs in at least one important aspect from the fatalism conventionally associated with premodernity. Rather than giving the future over to external, metaphysical forces, it is the self that becomes the idol; it is a fatalism based on trust in individuals' own competencies to deal with whatever life brings, to turn the fate of "contingency into destiny" (Heller and Feher 1988: 27). Garhammer puts it more directly still: "The renouncement of a systematic approach to one's own future is . . . the subjective complement to life trajectories that have become objectively more uncertain" (1999: 482–83).

Kurt Wolff's thoughts are pertinent here. Drawing on his earlier work *Surrender and Catch* (1976), he situates his notion of "surrender" in the uncertainties of the present. To "surrender" oneself to "a problem, an object, a situation" is in Wolff's view the best possible way to understand it; "for this reason," he notes, "human beings today are at their most rational in their surrender" (1998: 8–9). As far as my respondents are concerned, their fatalism, their surrender constitutes an attempt to "catch" the self. As Wolff puts it elsewhere: "[The idea of surrender-and-catch] takes the problematic character of traditional orientations and their institutions seriously by realizing and affirming that the self alone is the source of truth" (1983: 264). Indeed, the fatalism of these new adults is not so much, as Giddens (1991: 110) calls it, "the refusal of modernity—a repudiation of a controlling orientation to the future in favor of an attitude that lets events come as they will." On the contrary: it is precisely letting events come as they will that is the fitting controlling orientation, a rational response to prevailing social conditions.[1]

At times the respondents' faith in themselves, their belief in the possibility of the "catch," is so strong that even an awareness that the world at large is anything but a safe and secure place, that the actions of others, however removed in time and space, can have detrimental consequences, cannot shake it. Christopher, Karen, and Ethan voice what they perceive as negative instances with potential implications for the future: "I don't think we're working toward greater equality, which is something I do value highly. I see that as a huge problem . . . I do see the dependence of the developing on the first world as becoming increasingly worse, and the poor of the first world becoming increasingly third world. . . . And the erosion of a sense of solidarity really worries me because . . . the continuation of the world-being-about-me idea really scares the shit out of me. But I'm excited by the scope to be able to pursue things" (Christopher). "What scares me is what kind of a world . . . this [will] be . . . I'm optimistic because I know I can do a lot and maybe try and change things in a more positive way" (Karen). "I look at the world . . . and I wouldn't be surprised if our species was to extinguish itself pretty quickly. And that is not a pleasurable thought, but in some ways I'm less bothered about that. There is a possibility for some dignity within that" (Ethan). The more troubling aspects of life are external to the person. Vaguely conceived future contributions toward "making the world a better place," a belief in the capacity to marshal the self against all odds, and a quasi-religious redemptive vision serve here as imaginary (but no less real) defenses against external threats. It is not my intention to trivialize these very real concerns about the social environment; but it is worth pondering to what extent this presentation of an ethical self is a conversational idiom that serves as a social lubricant across the often widely differentiated social milieus in which these individuals operate. As such this "ethics of responsibility" may well be normative to new adults, and as such feeds back into the fatalistic bases of their stance toward life; and it may also function as a reminder that in principle, the selection of the right option at the right time (a time that may or may never come) will assuage existential threats.

The differentiation and individualization of horizons of opportunity sensitizes the imagination; present-centeredness is balanced with projections of self into a formless future where plans elude a firm grasp and remain unhinged.

Remaining Norms

As a social category the attainment of adulthood relies on the attainment, conferral, and "moral demand" (Goffman 1959: 13) of adult recognition, something that due to the diffuse nature of the prevalent dynamics of recognition is to a diminishing extent possible once and for all. This fluidity is, as I suggested, connected to historical, social, and cultural changes that have seen objective markers of adulthood that once permitted unambiguous distinctions to be made between adulthood and adolescence, lose universal validity. This does not augur the end of adulthood per se, but points to a redefinition of this social category; a redefinition to which the practices of some trendsetting young adults are vital. While in my discussion so far I have stressed the diminishing normative force of objectively identifiable adult achievements, this needs to be qualified. Although many young adults do not consider marriage, parenthood, a nine-to-five job central to their adult status, the fact remains that if one or more of these markers of adulthood are achieved, adult recognition, and thus self-recognition, is a quasiautomatic consequence. Gavin's entry into parenthood serves as an illustration against which others' adulthood can be brought into relief. For this reason his story warrants a more substantial reiteration and analysis.

First, Gavin talks about his life before the birth of his twin daughters, and he does so in a way that closely resembles other interviewees' descriptions of their present circumstances and attitudes: "I think the project of my self, that was it. I studied at university not out of desire for a degree at all; that was kind of a by-product of getting a degree. . . . Following whatever interested me kept me in that . . . very youthful state of mind, which I probably didn't realize was being youthful until I had children." He then relates a brief transitionary period that, with its final culmination in parenthood, reads like an illustration of what Schütz (1970) meant when he spoke of the "shock" that actors experience when they enter unfamiliar worlds—"finite provinces of meaning" for which the already acquired stock of knowledge proves, for a time at least, inadequate: "Two years ago I was pushed onto a fulltime [work] contract, which worked out well for me anyway. I sold both of my motorbikes, and I bought a car, a very sensible looking car. And I joked, "The universe is conspiring against me, something is going on." I got a fulltime job, I got a nice apartment, I'm driving a car that looks like a family car. Next thing you know we are pregnant with twins [laughs]. I joke a lot about it." This was the defining moment that, in his view, catapulted Gavin into adulthood: "We fell pregnant [and] decided to have the babies. . . . And that . . . for me was the critical thing that changed my attitude and since then my understanding of myself. . . . If anything defines adulthood for me, if anything was "change": now I feel like an adult." In contrast to the transitionary events and moments mentioned by others, this was not a retrospective, ad hoc attribution of meaning to a past event. Rather, the insight "now I feel like an adult" was cotemporaneous with the actual experience.

In Gavin's case the social significance of age norms is particularly evident. Always having been perceived as much younger due to his (verifiable and self-professed) young looks, he is aware of the authority that comes by virtue of looking more adult: "Going gray won't be bad for me. . . . The actual signs of aging [will] make my life easier for me, that socially ascribed authority that comes with it." At the same time, it is precisely this experience of always having looked younger than his age that makes his newly acquired adult status such a profound experience for him:

> That is why I'm having, in a sense, my first experience of adulthood now. I don't think I ever experienced adulthood before. Everything else was an abstract concept. When I gave a guest lecture or tutored and I'd look at it and go, "this is a good thing, this is very adult," you know. [But] that was never an experience. I was outside of myself looking at myself going, "I'm not feeling like an adult, it's not an embodied feeling," that's the difference. Now, for the first time in my life I actually am experiencing adulthood. That's a huge difference. For me, I would say that's the crux of the thing. I have reflected on many experiences that I've had that I thought were adult experiences, but not until now have I ever felt like an adult.

In fact, parenthood has alleviated some of his concerns regarding his appearance and how its meaning may be construed by others. The embodiment of adulthood Gavin talks about negates to a degree the embodiment of youth that has for years influenced many of his experiences with authority and was an integral part of his self-identification; "to a degree," because in the next sentence Gavin qualifies his thoughts, and in so doing illustrates how age norms compete with the objective markers of adulthood: "I can't experience adulthood fully partly because of my youthful appearance." Gavin's statements throughout the interview give the overall impression that this is an internal struggle that is of limited social significance when compared to his status as father; but it is present nevertheless as a very corporeal aspect of his self-perception that is constituted by the way others treat him.

Gavin's thoughts bring into sharp relief views articulated by the other respondents. For instance, the reasons given for the renouncement of the standard markers by other respondents are made without having experienced these status-conferring practices. Thus, imaginary forms of standard adulthood that are deduced from the interpretation of a previous generation's experiences take precedence over lived realities. And these imaginary representations consist largely of tropes that spell the end to an open-ended future full of unrealized potential, "the full-stop" many are "reluctant to apply," as Ethan put it. But Gavin's parent-hood did bring with it something new: a distinct feeling of integration into the adult world:

> My experience walking down the street is different because I'm aware of it [adult-hood] being a purely cultural concept now that I have children and I'm a father. I smile to myself, and, you know, there I am, still the same, dressing the same and everything like that, and looking the same—a little bit more tired than I used to, maybe not quite as youthful [laughs] but suddenly I felt connected, where I never felt that connection to society before, I had somehow felt outside society. . . . But then I guess becoming a parent changed that pretty radically.

The responsibility for the lives of others was indeed a big change for Gavin:

> I have to work and I have to earn money and I have to support this family. And that is the most practical thing that pushed me into adulthood. Now I have to think about maintaining a home, I have to think about their health and their education and . . . I have to provide for them not only week to week, but year to year. And so suddenly I have changed from, in a sense, celebrating change in my life and feel-ing that freedom that you do . . . [when you are] the project of . . . [your] life. Now I'm no longer the project of my life at all. It's there, the "making of yourself," it has remained for me, but it's so much subjugated to enjoying my family and looking after my kids.

The experience of adulthood as a tangible change in Gavin's status also meant that a haphazard drifting gave way to a more focused pragmatism whose motiva-tion lies decidedly outside the self. But, as will become clear below, Gavin too has an aversion to planning beyond the intermediate future, his newly acquired status notwithstanding. What does his having to take responsibility for others "not only week to week but year to year" mean for Gavin's attitude toward the future? For one, the sense of purpose he receives from his parental/adult status has brought about a change in his attitude to work: "I used to be pretty ambivalent about the future without really desiring anything. I didn't desire material wealth enough to go and chase it, to work hard towards a career that pays a lot. It's different [now], it's given me a reason to go and work and earn money, which is nice. . . . There's a bit of a whip there cracking me along. It's good for me, I think." On the other hand, his new responsibilities bring to the fore the necessity to plan ahead and the impossibility of meeting the financial burdens with which this is equated: "I think of planning, but the cost of planning for now is too much, I can't afford to plan. You know, where they [the kids] gonna go to school, what they gonna do. Just paying the bills is enough. . . . I can only think about it in economic terms, and it's negative. Ultimately, yes, the only chance I can really see ourselves of owning a house, or having that stability knowing that I could pay the rent on a place for years to come, would be winning lotto, and I don't buy lottery tickets." And again: "You can't plan; it seems impossible. It's hard to know what to plan for anyway. Because it suddenly becomes complicated. As soon as I go down the path of planning my future unravels anyway. . . . If I think about a plan, the plan is to be in a position where I don't have to plan. That'd be nice, not to worry about things." And just like his contemporaries, Gavin sees in the idea of planning a constraint he prefers to ignore, even though he is aware of his responsibilities: "Planning to me is something that is based on being subjugated to some force, whether it's poverty or the threat of poverty. . . . Planning itself becomes a symbol of that imprisonment, that loss of power, that loss of freedom . . . I guess it's something I don't want to let go of . . . freedom comes from not having to plan."

Gavin's case highlights the importance of experience for the attainment of adulthood—or, more precisely, a degree of certainty about one's passage toward it. Looking back upon his life, the advent of parenthood is the key marker of Gavin's transition. This is not something he planned; it was thrust upon him. But he identifies himself as adult because the (accidental) attainment of a classic marker of adulthood has brought his self-understanding closer to the standard notion of being fully grown up, of being like other more conventional grown-ups. This does suggest that the social force of a normative ideal strongly influences self-perception. Yet, this does not mean that Gavin was not an adult before becoming a father. Rather, the powerful emotional experience of parenthood, together with the social recognition of its significance, effected a drastic change in his outlook. This also precipitated the opening of an experiential gap between Gavin and his childless peers. Having attained one of the classic markers, his retrospective self-evaluation as nonadult before the birth of his daughters shows that Gavin now privileges the commensurability of experience with socially validated practice along conventional lines as marking full adult status. In so doing he implicitly attributes non-adulthood to others who do not have children. (We could speculate here to what extent similar evaluative strategies are at play where social scientists and media commentators are concerned.) Gavin's example points to the fact that there are different, albeit coexisting ways of being grown up. This includes the many twenty and thirtysomethings who fit the standard model more closely than the other new adults on whom my research focuses. The tensions that underscore the emergence of new norms are thus not simply a matter of generational difference, but also of the plural and differentiated quality of ways of life in contemporary modernity.

Self-Centeredness or Self-Centering?

A future that can be constructed beyond an intermediate stretch of time appears to these young adults as ultimately too constraining on their perceived biographical agency, awareness of structural insecurity, precariousness, and un-certainty notwithstanding. I suggest that it is in the perception of and their faith-like reliance on agency that their optimism resides. Becoming adult for these young people (Gavin being the exception) does not mean getting mar-ried, having kids, buying a house, or finding that one stable job. It means, above all, learning to handle themselves in different, changing contexts; becoming less susceptible to others' influence; striving toward self-knowledge and self-acceptance; learning to play the game; choosing values and principles that guide them through adult life, to steel themselves for "whatever." This they may well have learned from their baby boomer parents, who, particularly if they came from middle-class families, laid the groundwork for a more introspective and postmaterialist way of life. To be sure, it appears that these lessons are falling on more fertile ground today; their aims are much better suited to the contingen-cies of the present than to the background securities of the past.

A core belief that helps the respondents deal with the contingencies of con-temporary life is their belief in the necessity to be open to change, to flexibly adapt to the vicissitudes of their adulthood, to the unpredictability of social rela-tions. Growing up therefore also is a process of internalization of the uncertainty into which they were born. And being adult, finally, means to have successfully reconciled the uncertainty of the world they face with an advantageous stance toward it. To internalize flexibility as a way of life is to shun (or be at least suspi-cious of) the securing ties of long-term commitment even if they were available.

New adults' relative optimism concerning the future can thus be further con-textualized. For if being grown up means to have acquired the confidence and skills to adapt to uncertainty, then this also means that they have acquired the confidence and skills to mold and shape the one aspect of their world that is still predictable for all its plasticity, and over which they perceive having ultimate control: the self. The members of their generation posit themselves as malleable, flexible, and open to new experiences. Yet, rather than evidence for a burgeon-ing self-centeredness, these attitudes are symptomatic of something else: it is people's way to be adult in a different and historically unprecedented set of social circumstances that require a particular kind of self-centeredness; not so much an egoistic self-centeredness marked by disinterest in others that reproduces a "culture of narcissism," but a self-centering. In the process of becoming adults, these individuals gradually come to realize that the only center that promises stability lies within. This is the latent rationale that often lies behind remarks such as "[growing up means] taking responsibility for yourself . . . first and fore-most" (Isabelle); or, "If something upsets you then change it. Make it better for you. You gotta look after number one and that's yourself" (Anthony). Indeed, the social category "adulthood" is heavily invested with a psychological vocabulary. It appears that the respondents compensate for the increasingly abstract nature of standard adulthood by recourse to a language that signifies things that are no less intangible and yet have become part of everyday discourse: personal development and growth, "realizing your potential," "being true to yourself," "putting number one first," "accepting me," and so on. From another perspective this has been called "individualism of self-fulfillment" (Taylor 1991). The pop psychology of "therapy culture" (Furedi 2004), it seems, furnishes a set of readily available ideas that people draw upon to think about themselves. Hence, adulthood too is most easily described in these terms. And so, while some forms of adult experiences were and are mediated by socially validated markers, others lack this particular kind of mediation; what takes its place is a turn to the self. We cannot discount the possibility that this self-directedness has salutary aspects:

> Now we have a cultural attempt to deal with adulthood, to develop a set of myths and images that can give moral meaning and purpose to a life that has no fixed end, no dramatic conclusion. In some ways the reaction to this challenge seems to be a culture of narcissism, in which the self and its perpetuation become all, in which the trick is to remain alive and whole without risking attachment or making binding choices. But the other side of these cultural explorations is a search for models of self . . . that are compatible with continuing growth and change, that permeate with moral significance the ups and downs of daily life, the struggle to live well, rather than giving moral meaning only to the dramatic moment of the shift from youth to adulthood. (Swidler 1980: 144)

These remarks capture well the significance of the redefinition of contemporary adulthood to individual lives and, by extension, to the sociological enterprise. They constitute a fitting end to the main body of my exploration. With this, and by way of summary, I turn to some concluding remarks.

7

CONCLUSION:
REDEFINING ADULTHOOD

Contemporary young adults have grown up in a world that is very different from the world in which their parents came of age, and so their adulthoods are very different. Yet, for that they are often upbraided by some whose point of view is influenced by experiences that were framed in social and cultural conditions that by and large no longer obtain. At times it is suggested that many individuals of the younger generation are failing to take responsibility for their lives, and social scientists (not always unwittingly) supply arguments that serve to legitimate pejorative judgments about these people. Perhaps Herant Katchadourian (1978: 55) was right when he suggested, "We assume young people to be what is convenient to adults for them to be and we then get upset when they are not." I have argued in the preceding chapters that these judgments are misinformed because the changing meaning of adulthood, the central evaluative category, is not adequately taken into account.

The waning of the classic markers' empirical validity and normative force has made this task a complex one; and the dominance of an excessively individualizing social-psychological view that time and again is reproduced in public forums and feeds ambiguous self-perceptions constituted a formidable challenge to my task. I began by delineating the delayed adulthood thesis, a conceptual amalgam of different approaches to young people's practices centered on the belief that many of today's twenty and thirtysomethings defer or reject adulthood, and then went on to show that the evaluative benchmark against which such conclusions are formulated is outdated; it represents the adulthood of another generation and another era. Yet, this anachronistic model contains important clues to my elaboration of an alternative perspective. The classic features of adulthood were markers of adulthood during the immediate postwar period precisely because they were eminently realizable; all who attained them were socially recognized as adults because what people did, and when they did it, was strongly connected to the attitudes they held, to who they were. These adults in turn valued those criteria as signifying more than material possessions, stability, or commitment: as the social expressions of maturity they signified full personhood. During that time the idea of adulthood was clear, taken for granted, and entrenched in the social imagination—and thus remained by and large unarticulated. This template was valid as, for a while, it was commensurate with prevailing social circumstances.

In the past three decades a normative lag has opened up between this ideal model and the practices and orientations of many individuals. This lag lies at the heart of orthodox, normative assumptions. Social scientists, commentators, journalists, and marketers alike perceive the nonattainment or deferral of the classic markers of adulthood as a kind of behavioral deviance from the norm, while the norm itself remains uncontested. But the rejection, refusal, or deferral of a particular vision of adulthood is only part of the story. People are, in fact, redefining the very meaning of adulthood. Adulthood is more than individuals' state of mind, more than a matter of self-perception. Just as the standard model is evidence of the social nature of what it means to be grown up (and therefore has now become inappropriate), so the present-day remodeling of adulthood must draw its social meaning from current circumstances.

Whether with respect to the standard model or emergent forms, recognition of individuals as full members of society is the meaningful constant of adulthood; it is the common denominator of the standard model as well as of the new adulthood. The difference between these forms of adulthood is marked by changes in the social processes that frame how and on what basis adult recognition is constituted. This difference can be traced as a shift from the social recognition of stability in the past to the social recognition of flexibility in the present. However, with respect to the latter there is an important proviso: because the traditional model of adulthood persists as an ideal, personal orientations and practices that are best suited to contemporary relations of recognition are insufficiently acknowledged. Thus, the normative lag leads to a recognition deficit.

There are two reasons for this recognition deficit. First, at the level of everyday and social scientific discourse, there is a misunderstanding of young people's manner of social integration. Second, young people themselves feel ambivalent about the standard model of adulthood. While they may recognize it as an ideal, they may at the same time remain doubtful about how far they are succeeding—or wanting to succeed—in its realization. At first glance, this poses a dilemma for my proposition that the so-called kidults of today are in fact adults, particularly as I also work with the proposition that recognition is entwined with integration. One way out of this dilemma is to acknowledge that this type of integration is not attained once-and-for-all. The very criteria upon which adult recognition rests are not static. Rather, they depend on the social milieus to which they apply. Flexibility as a way of life, a central contemporary existential orientation, implies both the capacity to attain social recognition across plural and often quite different social environments and the ability to cope with changes within them. In fact, as the interview material shows, the respondents are aware that they need to fulfill different expectations in a number of different social environments. The new adulthood is marked by the pluralization of the terms of reference that delimit its meaning by dint of a shift from monolithic prescription to a plurality of values and orientations that are drawn upon in diverse contexts. This can mean that performances that mimic conventional expectations are perceived in terms of inauthenticity, something that pertains particularly to the objective aspects of their adulthood. On the other hand, contemporary adults generally consider themselves full persons because they lead ethical lives together with others in whatever domain of social life. This is the part of their subjectivity perceived in terms of authenticity. In a sense, then, they are caught between two adulthoods. Their adulthood is a kind of balancing act of personal self-understanding, social expectations, and the need for a life of one's own. That, however, does not prevent them from being responsible, committed, independent human beings, no matter how attached the notions of responsibility, commitment, and independence are to the classic markers of adulthood. In fact, their redefinition of adulthood on the level of practice ushers in a redefinition of the evaluative criteria that for so long have been attributed to these normative behaviors.

The new adulthood is distinguished from the standard model by a loss of telos. Structural uncertainties, the demand for flexibility, the openness of future time horizons, and the centrality of personal growth imbue the new adulthood with a quality that confounds conventional understandings of maturity as a goal: it is perpetually liminal; it has no definite destination. This liminality is further buttressed by the social imperative of youthfulness, a phenomenon that provides the ideological framework for dynamics of recognition that prevail in conditions of advanced market capitalism. As such, the proclivities and practices of many people in their twenties and thirties—evidence of a lack of maturity in the eyes of some—are in fact well suited to the pluralized social contingencies of the present. This, as we have seen, is rarely acknowledged. Dissenting voices are rare, though there are signs that as adulthood is redefined, observers of that process too are appearing. Like this volume, they address these changes by reembedding individual lives in their social context. And as this alternative view gains more prominence, supported by further research of a slowly congealing community of like-minded scholars and commentators, the feedback loop between common-sense thinking and intellectual work will inevitably gain momentum. As a result, the process of redefinition will receive discursive recognition and open up avenues for the expression of different lives, different adulthoods, unburdened by old prejudices. Hence, full recognition of new forms of adulthood—the bridging of the normative lag, the rollback of the current recognition deficit—are subject to a willingness to engage with new adults as adults in their own right. To an extent, though, this will be an inevitable outcome of the natural generational turnover.

Generations, Inheritance, Responsibility

My inquiry into the redefinition of adulthood elucidated the normative productivity of social practices. Intergenerational relationships bear significantly on these issues. The new adults' parents asserted their adulthood against the authority of their own parents, against their predecessors. To this end their cultural productions, taken up and driven along by the culture industry, provided for strong generational identifications. These were bolstered by a political awareness galvanized by Cold War crises, the Vietnam War, and in the United States, the Civil Rights struggle. These currents, even for those who did not identify directly with them, nevertheless normatively circumscribed what it meant to be young in the 1960s and early 1970s, namely *not* to identify with the parent generation.

Today the once asymmetric relations between parents and children are waning. And while it is not my intention to detract from the violent realities that continue to blight many an intergenerational relationship, the channels of communication between children and parents are generally more open than in a past when more authoritarian, top-down approaches prevailed. Furthermore, cultural and aesthetic identifications tend toward similarity as well as difference. The music and fashions of younger adults often contain significant stylistic elements borrowed from the recycled products of their parents' teenage years. The crux, however, is this: today individuation no longer necessarily occurs *against* that which parents used to represent for the young, that is, gatekeepers of the status quo, conservatism, obsolescence. Instead, individuation has to occur more exclusively within macrosocial realities, which were to a significant degree furnished *by* the parent generation. The phenomenon of "youth rebellion," so significant for a generation that came of age in the 1950s, '60s, and '70s, appears to have vanished or at least to have been confined to aesthetic self-expression and identification.

It is under these changed conditions for individuation that the biographical primacy of personal development makes further sense. New adults actually deploy the cultural and subjective resources that they inherited from their parents in a world that fosters such orientations. Ideals of self-exploration and discovery that gained mass appeal during the baby boomers' coming of age are perhaps only now meeting the conditions necessary for their complete assimilation as taken-for-granted aspects of contemporary life conduct. That is, the parents' bohemian ideals constitute the children's mundane reality in times of uncertainty, while the mundane reality of those who came of age in times of stability represents no more than a collection of residuals ideal that is regarded with ambivalence by new adults. Put differently, existing opportunities in the economic boom era meant that for some self-exploration and development were often a temporary lifestyle choice before entry into standard adulthood. But today, in a world of no guarantees the turn to the self is no longer extraordinary, nor is it associated with a counterculture. The centrality of personal growth and fulfillment is marked by its utter ordinariness; it is a normal and necessary part of many new adults' frame of mind, even a habitual conversational idiom. Thus the new fatalism has its source not only in the social conditions into which new adults were born, but also in an orientation to life that was passed to them in the cradle.

This mentality also happens to be highly commensurate with the present-day emphasis on "choice" in the policy arena and on election rostrums—the kind of rhetoric that divests governments of responsibility, and invests individuals with increasing self-accountability even and especially regarding things that used to be public goods (health, education, social welfare, infrastructure). Just as demand and supply are interdependent in the market of goods, so attitudes and promises feed off each other in the market of ideas, ideologies, and political power. Make no mistake: the new adults of today are also the inheritors of a world shaped to a significant degree by the Reagans and the Thatchers; the Hawkes, Keatings, and Howards; the Bushes, Blairs, and Schröders. They are the subjects of neoclassical economics; of neoliberalism as political ideology, social program, and practice—people, that is, whose social environments were prepared for them by the same generation that would often like to see them grow up the way they once did. Is it not remarkable then, we may ask ourselves, that the new adults of today are mostly not the selfish, rational, utility-maximizing individuals that would, finally, embody and personify the fulfilled wishes of many an economist and politician? Is it not astonishing that in so many ways they usually manage to live, work, and love just like other generations have: with a good measure of self-respect and concern for others?

There are many open questions here that a study of this sort can no more than hint at. But on the issue of self-respect we might, for example, ponder the criteria for adult recognition that are withheld from those who, unlike the respondents, fall outside mainstream political and cultural discourses, who are in crucial ways misrecognized and disrespected for their gender, sexualities, age, cultural and religious backgrounds, or economic and legal marginality. In a sense, these people make up the foil that reflects the issues with which I have dealt here. By way of example, picture a woman in her late twenties, unemployed, and with a career of petty crime and entries to and exits from state institutions. Her citizenship rights have for some periods been revoked; her labor market chances are immeasurably slim in comparison to your average tertiary educated citizen. Some would say she has forfeited those chances; others contend that unduly punitive systems shut down avenues for the betterment of her life chances. Her values and practices do not concord with what constitutes a productive "full partner in interaction" in the social order writ large. And yet, she is not a child. If she was to pass me in the street I would not judge her to be a child. She may feel adult because she has had to deal with situations that most of us are protected from. But her adulthood, her personhood, depends in crucial ways on her relationships with others, others that may help her and guide her as well as others that keep the bar raised sufficiently high to render life an unceasing trial. This, I admit, is haphazard speculating and points in other research directions. Yet, this vignette nevertheless indicates the ethical underpinnings of adulthood as a social category: the positive self-evaluation of every individual's personhood is not simply a cognitive logic played out in a hermetically sealed black box; it is collectively constituted and thus a responsibility all of us share.

Social Change and Social Theory

Many social theorists evaluate social change in terms of a cultural decline. Often this is evidence of academics' ability to articulate that which is keenly felt by others. Sometimes, and especially in relation to the topic of this book, it betrays a certain nostalgia for a time in which things were different, when coming of age seemed more uncomplicated, even qualitatively better. It is quite possible that negative evaluations of social change have played a part in sociology's lack of serious concern with adulthood, in addition to tacitly supporting the position from which a judgmental gaze upon the younger generation is being cast. Now, I have argued here that the young people of today—and by implication, the adults of the future—are and will be different from the mature individuals of an era when adulthood was an unproblematic social fact. In putting this forward, my analysis has not been discontinuous with extant ideas. Indeed, it is not my intention to criticize important social analyses, or to substitute them with a facile optimism. My thoughts are provoked, above all, by a curiosity about how individuals and societies manage to go on; how we continue to make sense of the world, let alone manage to cooperate; how and where we find realms of freedom in light of the many dire diagnoses that have accompanied the study of social change, and especially the study of young people.

Sociologists have from time to time marveled at the fact that there is no "sociology of adulthood." Here is my take on this situation. The default status of adulthood means that sociologists constantly reproduce the concept as a disciplinary, intersubjectively constituted yet undertheorized given. It is precisely this tacit (though pivotal) role that has enabled the meaning of adulthood to elude analysis. Yet it is possible that, should its meaning become subject to analysis, as a concept it would remain marginal to sociology. Adulthood would then be subsumed as part of a subdisciplinary enterprise even though its unquestioned acceptance has so far been vital to almost everything sociologists do. That is to say, little would change: this new sociology of adulthood would take care of theory building and applied research, while the rest of the field would go on assuming adult beliefs and practices as the invisible backdrop to social inquiry in general. Furthermore, investigating the meaning of adulthood as a socially constructed idea potentially threatens a firmly established parameter of analysis. Research into young people's transition to adulthood is one example. In acknowledging that the destination at transition's end is conceptually contestable, one puts the very notion of transition into question. But at the same time, it is particularly vital to conceptually ground adulthood because of the importance of social research into young people's trajectories from education to work, and the investment the discipline has in "youth transitions" as a viable area. On this account I invite others to think and rethink present perspectives and approaches. Still, one thing is clear. Adulthood as a distinct field of sociological investigation has something to offer. Investigating different modes of adulthood offers the possibility to question the distribution of opportunities and to plot the possibilities for social recognition, and thus for individuation and emancipation, in different, plural, and pluralizing milieus.

To address the dynamics of social recognition is to take important cues from the rich source of critical theory—the basis of the recognition-theoretical turn in contemporary sociology and social philosophy. I cannot pretend to have done justice to this tradition here, though I hope to have been able to infuse my research with its critical spirit. To avoid elevating the adulthood of another generation to something it can for many no longer represent implies scrutinizing existing social conditions and actual opportunities; acknowledging the precariousness and changeability of contemporary social relations; and, perhaps, to begin envisaging institutional arrangements that may better provide existential securities under conditions of more apparent and more unpredictable flux than has been the case in the past.

Present practices must be judged in their present social context. That is not to say that the past should be ignored. On the contrary, analyzing the social conditions of previous generations' coming of age can tell us much about changes in structures of opportunity and the way individuals negotiate the ebbs and flows of their biographies. However, judging the practices of the present by the standards of the past leads to the conceptual disembedding of individual lives from their actual social context.

The new adulthood of today is no better or worse than the adulthood of previous generations; that individuals are bound to the social conditions in which they find themselves and which they co-create, while at the same time they create the normative frame that enables them to become full partners in interaction. They do this as best they can, wherever they can, and with as much dignity as they can muster. The new young adults of today may be without a center that holds. But, they are no more and no less than matchless actors in times of uncertainty.

Epilogue

❧

On a seasonably hot summer's day I find myself mingling with a wedding crowd in an inner-city Sydney suburb. The bride looks radiant, the bridegroom nervous. A one-year-old is passed from bride to bridesmaid and then on to her grandmother. Things have indeed changed for Louise since the time of the interview. There is a strong feeling on her part that giving birth, being a mother, and getting married are threshold experiences that render erstwhile confusions as to what adulthood meant ("Adulthood sort of ends up a big mish-mash.") a distant, barely fathomable state of mind. Her clearly articulated need for anchorage has dissolved; she has become the anchor for someone else.

Christopher, for whom wish fulfillment was "the death of future," had only just met his new partner at the time of the interview. Soon afterward he consented to his girlfriend's proposal for marriage. They are now married and are traveling Australia for a while without any firm ideas about their journey's end. The future is still full of possibilities; and while it is still as full of promise as it was some three years ago, he will face it with someone he loves deeply. Christopher and his partner are conscious that their relationship is until-further-notice simply because "you never know what happens in the future." One gets the feeling that in the knowledge and acknowledgement of the future's unpredictability lies the key to and the hope for a long life together.

Isabelle has been busy climbing the corporate ladder since I saw her last. Now she is planning on having a child, if possible this year. With her partner of eight years she has recently bought her first house. Back in 2002 her adulthood was "first and foremost" about being responsible for herself. Something has changed. The adulthood "out there"—an ideal whose realization was for all of Isabelle's self-directedness a clearly delineated model—is becoming more and more, it seems, the adulthood "in here." The two adulthoods are on a course toward reconciliation.

Fred, who was so conscious of personal politics as a part of adulthood, and who saw adulthood very much in instrumental, purposive terms, is making a career—

in politics, no less. David has embarked on doctoral studies in sociology, which have taken him overseas twice for fieldwork. He continues to live with his parents and is devoted to the same woman with whom he had entered into a relationship not long before the interview. He has yet to get his driver's license, I am told. Only recently I came across Michelle in a local shopping mall, where she now works as a shop assistant after having given up her studies on the halfway mark. She is still belly dancing though and appears to have found her niche.

What are we to make of these stories? Have Louise, Christopher, Isabelle, and Fred only now entered adulthood, or at least come closer to its realization? What about Anthony, Greg, David, and Michelle? Is their adulthood caught in a state of emergence, awaiting achievement, resolution, actualization? I think not. For those who have embarked on the realization of the more entrenched markers of adulthood this may well presage subjective feelings of achievement—they are acutely aware of milestones. But there is cognizance that recognition on some levels—as committed, responsible persons—no longer predicates certainty in other domains of life, and that valuing one's own personhood and the person-hood of others no longer hinges on the external markers of the past. The precari-ous balance of work and home life, children's education as well as financial fu-tures remain pressing concerns. Incertitude is not assuaged; added responsibilities crowd the realm of freedom, the intimate sphere, their loves. They may never emerge into an adulthood the way this social category is commonly understood. But they will, so it seems, pull through regardless. Whatever the case may be, faith in the self permits of no alternative scenario.

Finally. This is the place where the illusions of social scientific objectivity are more consciously put aside. I met adults some years ago, and met them again of late. Their journeys in all their ordinariness are remarkable. They are the stories of which my ideas are spun and whose spirit deserves not disparagement, but no less than respect and recognition for new adulthoods well lived.

NOTES

Notes to the Introduction

1. Theorists deploy the concept of "recognition" not in order to denote the identification of an object through prior knowledge, but as a synonym for the German *Anerkennung*. As such it connotes social validation, approbation, approval, or acknowledgement. This is the sense in which the term is used throughout this volume.

2. I say "allegedly" because I have to date been unable to unearth the precise locus of Freud's much-quoted, but, as it appears, never referenced phrase.

3. I variously refer to "new adults," "new adulthood," and "contemporary young adults." Johanna Wyn and Peter Dwyer, from whom I borrow the term, use "new adulthood" in the context of their studies of young Australians born after 1970 (e.g., Dwyer and Wyn 2001: 2; Wyn 2004). In a similar manner, I understand new adults to be members of a generation born into a world already sufficiently changed by the effects of a neoclassical economic accord and neoliberal political consensus to warrant another descriptor that separates them from previous generations. Because the protagonists share a postcompulsory education and thus relatively good life chances, they often have more in common with similarly positioned individuals in other societies (developed and less developed) than with many in their own. However, I do—emphatically—not intend to label yet another species of adult, or another generation, and least of all a distinct cohort because the new adulthood—commensurate with the social conditions of the present—is emergent and ever-changing. Likewise, I attribute no particular analytical value to the term "young adults" other than trusting in a shared common sense that distinguishes young from old. For a discussion of the term's theoretical yield, see the European Group for Integrated Social Research (EGRIS 2001).

Notes to Chapter 1

1. The original quotation is, "the immaturity of children is a biological fact of life but the ways in which this immaturity is understood and made meaningful is a fact of culture" (James and Prout 1997: 7).

2. However, as Merser reminds us, we should bear in mind that what became the standard for normal adulthood was "statistically as well as practically abnormal," as "at no point, in American history at least, did people marry and establish households as young as they did in the 1950s and 1960s" (1978: 68; 72).

3. At the same time, in the echelons of Western leadership the notion "peace impossible, war unlikely" prevailed at home (Aron 1966)—while havoc was wreaked in what was then known as Indochina. For a fascinating political history of the Cold War, see Martin Walker (1994).

4. For an authoritative and comprehensive Western history of the "long Sixties" from about 1958 to approximately 1974, see Marwick (1999).

5. The mean duration of marriages among OECD countries in 1999 was 10.4 years. The mean number of divorces has increased from 16 per 100 marriages in 1970, to 41 in 2000. There are significant variations between countries, however. The Catholic countries Italy and Ireland had fewer than 20 divorces per 100 marriages, while Austria, Belgium, Finland, Sweden, the United Kingdom, and the United States had 50 divorces and above per 100 marriages (Tiffen and Gittins 2004: 190–91).

6. Philippe Ariès, commenting on the rise of the date of birth for matters of identification, has this to say: "The Christian name belongs to the world of fancy, the surname to that of tradition. The age, a quantity legally measurable to within a few hours, comes from another world, that of precise figures. In our day our registration practices partake at the same time of all worlds" (1973: 13).

7. However, in Australia there is a "rebuttable presumption" deeming children between ten and less than fourteen years of age incapable of committing crimes (*doli incapax*). Only if it can be shown that the child is of considerable psychological maturity and was able to distinguish between right and wrong at the time the offense was committed, can a trial lead to conviction. Full responsibility for criminal acts comes into force between the ages of fourteen and eighteen, depending on jurisdiction. Also, young offenders are subject to a range of criminal sanctions that differ from adult sanctions for the same offense (Urbas 2000).

8. For an important critique of media representations of "kidults," see Crawford (2006).

9. For a detailed review of Côté's volume, see Blatterer (2003).

Notes to Chapter 2

1. The classic text of this thesis is Jacob Burckhardt's *The Civilization of the Renaissance in Italy* (1990 [1860]). For an alternative proposition see Colin Morris's thought-provoking study *The Discovery of the Individual, 1050—1200* (1995).

2. Honneth refers here to a study by Alain Ehrenberg (2004) that traces the emergence of depression (and its medicalization) as a social phenomenon. Ehrenberg argues convincingly that depression replaced neurosis, the central concern of psychoanalysis in the nineteenth century. Just as neurosis was linked to repression, depression is said to arise with having to be oneself as a cultural norm.

3. Bauman pays homage to W.B. Yeats. In "The Second Coming" (1991) [1921] the poet muses: "Things fall apart; the centre cannot hold."

4. Warde (2002) in his critique of Beck, Giddens, and Bauman, rejects undue emphasis on the connection between the overabundance of consumer goods, identity formation, and anxiety. He distinguishes between "choice" requiring the taking of responsibility and thus containing the possibility of anxiety, and more or less random "selection" undertaken with a blasé attitude.

5. In the same way that *le mal de mer* is seasickness—illness, discomfort, bad feeling caused by the motion of the water—*le mal de l'infini* may be loosely translated as "infinity sickness." I am reminded here of the beginning of Freud's *Das Unbehagen in der Kultur* (2004 [1930]), where he refers to his correspondence with Romain Rolland, who, according to Freud believed religiosity to be innate to humans. Its source is a sense, or a feeling (Empfindung) for eternity, a feeling of "something unlimited, unbounded, verily 'oceanic,'" which is both channeled and usurped by religious systems (2004: 31). For Freud, who admitted to be unable

to find such feelings within himself, but did not repudiate their existence offhand, this was perhaps to do with an unconscious memory of early infancy when subject and object are not yet sufficiently differentiated.

6. At the same time, referring to Ehrenberg's research, Honneth makes the point that the "transformation of the ideal of self-realization into an external constraint" may well be a contributing factor to depression as a mass phenomenon (Honneth 2002a: 156).

7. This was, for Durkheim, no more than a "preliminary definition" of a whole range of qualitatively nuanced social phenomena (Lukes 1992: 11). In his preface to the second edition of *The Rules* Durkheim distances himself from the narrow notion of constraint. He makes the case in one of his footnotes: "The coercive power that we contribute to it is so far from being the whole of the social fact that it can present the opposite character equally well. Institutions may impose themselves upon us, but we cling to them; they compel us, and we love them; they constrain us, and we find our welfare in our adherence to them and in this very constraint" (1966: lvi).

8. John Stuart Mill recognized that "plans of life" are a central aspect of individuality, but was keenly aware that their realization was subject to contingencies that elude rational design (Appiah 2005: 6–9). Rather than a conscious and explicit elaboration of future actions and goals, I take life planning in the broad sense to denote a meaningful connection of the present, past, and future.

9. The term "life cycle," which originates from biology and developmental psychology, no longer holds currency in the social sciences, where it has been replaced by "life course." This is so because the older notion universalizes a culturally specific sequence of life stages and therefore does not allow for cultural and historical variations concerning the social meaning of age and life expectancy (Pilcher 1995: 17–18). For an overview of the once-dominant ages and stages approach in psychology, see Rosenfeld and Stark (1987).

10. Campbell and Burgess (2001) discuss and undertake the integration of "casual employment"— the Australian version of temporary employment—into the existing OECD model. Casual work may include various work situations including long-term regular employment. However, its most distinctive feature is the absence of standard employment benefits in addition to issues of temporal insecurities. In contrast to most European countries, in Australia labor market deregulation during the 1990s was specifically aimed at dismantling those policies that protected permanent employees (e.g., through the establishment of *individual* Enterprise Agreements in place of collectively negotiated awards). In 2005, new Industrial Relations policies, peddled as "Work Choices," further undermine the remaining remnants of work securities, such as leave entitlements and employees' recourse to unfair dismissal legislation.

11. As a further step in the flexibilization of work may be cited McDonald's "Family Contract," which is currently being tested in the U.K. This allows family members to share one job and swap shifts at their leisure (*Sydney Morning Herald* 2006).

12. It must be noted here that at least in the United States traditional understandings of romantic love and marriage have not lost their normative status, the increasing prevalence of alternative arrangements notwithstanding (for an overview and interpretation of relevant studies, see Gross 2005).

13. Richard Sennett's (1998) suggestion that the successful building of character rests on the ability for long-term self-projection is an example of this line of thought.

14. For example, of the 2.5 million people employed in part-time jobs in Australia in 2001, 24 percent wanted fulltime employment, but were unable to attain it (ABS 2001b).

15. An Australian study of human resource managers' attitudes toward potential employees showed that of 500 HR personnel, not one would consider a male over 50 years of age employable (*Sydney Morning Herald* 2000). This is just one example of the centrality of age to what appears to be the enduring force of ascription in contemporary society.

Notes to Chapter 3

1. For a detailed, critical appreciation of Hegel's philosophical conception of recognition in several of his writings, see Williams (1997).
2. This proposition should not be stretched too far, however. Compensation must be understood in terms of relative equivalence: "You cannot, to give an example, compensate for being useless on the labor market by being a good [amateur] tennis player" (Honneth in Petersen and Willig 2002: 272).

Notes to Chapter 4

1. In fact, a lack of money is cited as the main reason why the beginnings of a U.S. youth culture "dried up in the Depression years" (Hine 1999: 226). On the spending habits of teenagers in the late 1950s, see Marwick (1999: 45–47).
2. "Work for the Dole" is an Australian Government initiative whereby unemployed individuals between the ages of eighteen and twenty-four are obliged to work a certain amount of hours per week in order to legitimate their benefits entitlement. For a succinct summary and critique see Pike (1997).

Notes to Chapter 5

1. For example, in the OECD there is a marked shift in labor force participation along the gender divide. While none of these countries can as yet boast an equal participation of men and women, the mean male participation has fallen by nine points from 1960 to 1999, while women's participation has increased by eighteen points during the same period (Tiffen and Gittins 2004: 68–69).

Notes to Chapter 6

1. I subscribe to Wolff's interpretation when, in the spirit of Max Weber, he points out that "rational" is here taken to mean substantive rather than instrumental or functional rationality (1998: 9).

BIBLIOGRAPHY

ABS (Australian Bureau of Statistics). 2000. "Family Formation: Young Adults Living in Parental Home." In *Social Trends*. Canberra: Australian Bureau of Statistics.

———. 2001a. *Western Australian Statistical Indicators*. Canberra: Australian Bureau of Statistics.

———. 2001b. "Underemployed Workers, Australia." Canberra: Australian Bureau of Statistics.

———. 2003. *Population by Age and Sex, Australian States and Territories*. Canberra: Australian Bureau of Statistics.

———. 2004a. *Year Book Australia*. Canberra: Australian Bureau of Statistics.

———. 2004b. "Births, Australia." Canberra: Australian Bureau of Statistics.

ACIRRT (Australian Centre for Industrial Relations Research and Training). 1999. *Australia at Work: Just Managing*. Sydney: Prentice Hall.

ACIRRT (Australian Centre for Industrial Relations Research and Training), and CEDA (Committee for Economic Development of Australia). 2002. "Health of the Labour Market Index." <http://acirrt.com.au> (19 April 2003).

Adorno, Theodor W. 1978. *Minima Moralia: Reflections from Damaged Life*, trans. E.F.N. Jephcott, London: New Left Books.

———. 2000. *Introduction to Sociology*, trans. E.F.N. Jephcott, ed. C. Gödde. Cambridge: Polity.

———. 2002. *The Culture Industry*, ed. J.M. Bernstein. London: Routledge.

AIC (Australian Institute of Criminology). 2003. "Age of Criminal Responsibility." *Juvenile Justice In Australia*. <http://www.aic.gov.au/ research/justice/html> (23 April 2004).

Allman, Lawrence R. 1982. *Readings in Adult Psychology: Contemporary Perspectives*, ed. L.R. Allman and D.T. Jaffe. New York: Harper and Row.

Appiah, Kwame Anthony. 2005. *The Ethics of Identity*. Princeton: Princeton University Press.

Ariès, Philippe. 1973. *Centuries of Childhood: A Social History of Family Life*. London: Cape.

Arnett, Jeffrey J. 1997. "Young People's Conceptions of the Transition to Adulthood." *Youth and Society* 29, no. 1: 3–21.

———. 1998. "Learning to Stand Alone: The Transition to Adulthood in Contemporary America in Cultural and Historical Context." *Human Development* 41, no. 5: 295–315.

———. 2000a. "Emerging Adulthood: A Theory of Development From the Late Teens Through The Twenties." *American Psychologist* 55, no. 5: 469–80.

———. 2000b. "High Hopes in a Grim World: Emerging Adults' Views of Their Futures and 'Generation X'" *Youth and Society* 31, no. 3: 267–86.

———. 2004. *Emerging Adulthood: The Winding Road from the Late Teens Through the Twenties*. New York: Oxford University Press.

Arnett, Jeffrey J., and Susan Taber. 1994. "Adolescence Terminable and Interminable: When Does It End?" *Journal Of Youth And Adolescence* 23: 517–39.

Aron, Raymond. 1966. *Peace and War: A Theory of International Relations*, trans. R. Howard and A.B. Fox. London: Weidenfeld and Nicholson.

Australian. 2001. "Now Wait Til 35 for Coming of Age." September 3.

———. 2004. "Kid, You'll be an Adult at 30." August 2.

Bauman, Zygmunt. 1990. *Thinking Sociologically*. Oxford and Cambridge: Blackwell.

———. 1995. "Searching for a Centre that Holds." In *Global Modernities*, ed. M. Featherstone, S. Lash, and R. Robertson. London: Sage.

———. 2000. *Liquid Modernity*. Cambridge: Polity.

———. 2001a. *The Individualized Society*. Cambridge: Polity.

———. 2001b. "The Great War of Recognition." *Theory, Culture & Society* 18, no. 2–3: 137–50.

———. 2003. *Liquid Love: On the Frailty of Human Bonds*. Cambridge: Polity.

BBC News. 2001. "Parental Hand-Outs Never Stop." <http://news.bbc.co.uk/1/hi/business/1459261. stm> (23 December 2005).

Beck, Ulrich. 1992. *Risk Society: Towards a New Modernity*, trans. M. Ritter. London: Sage.

———. 1997. *Kinder der Freiheit*. Frankfurt: Suhrkamp.

———. 2000. *The Brave New World of Work*. Cambridge: Polity.

Beck, Ulrich, and Elisabeth Beck-Gernsheim. 1995. *The Normal Chaos of Love*, trans. M. Ritter and J. Wiebel. Cambridge: Polity.

———. 2002. *Individualization: Institutional Individualism and its Social and Political Consequences*. London: Sage.

Beck, Ulrich, Anthony Giddens, and Scott Lash. 1994. Reflexive Modernisation: Politics, Tradition and Aesthetics in the Modern Social Order. Cambridge: Polity.

Berger, Peter. 1966. *An Invitation to Sociology: A Humanistic Perspective*. Harmondsworth: Penguin.

Berger, Peter, and Thomas Luckmann. 1971. *The Social Construction of Reality: A Treatise in the Sociology of Knowledge*. London: Penguin.

Berger, Peter, Brigitte Berger, and Hansfried Kellner. 1973. *The Homeless Mind: Modernization and Consciousness*. Harmondsworth: Penguin.

Bernstein, Basil B. 1977. *Class, Code and Control*. Vol. 3. London: Routledge and Kegan Paul.

Bischof, Ledford J. 1976. *Adult Psychology*. New York: Harper and Row.

Bittman, Michael, and Jocelyn Pixley. 1997. *The Double Life of the Family: Myth, Hope, and Experience*. Sydney: Allen and Unwin.

Blatterer, Harry. 2003. "Review: James Côté, Arrested Adulthood: The Changing Nature of Maturity and Identity." *Journal of Sociology* 39, no. 3: 308–12.

Blos, Peter. 1941. *The Adolescent Personality: A Study of Individual Behavior for the Commission on Secondary School Curriculum of the Progressive Education Association*. New York: Appleton.

Boëthius, Ulf. 1995. "Youth, Media and Moral Panics." *Youth Culture in Late Modernity*, ed. J. Fornäs and G. Bolin. London: Sage.

Bourdieu, Pierre. 1993. "'Youth' is Just a Word." In *Sociology in Question*. London: Sage.

———. 1998. "Job Insecurity is Everywhere Now." In *Acts of Resistance*. Cambridge: Polity.

Buchmann, Marlis. 1989. *The Script of Life in Modern Society: Entry into Adulthood in a Changing World*. Chicago: University of Chicago Press.

Burckhardt, J. 1990 [1860]. *The Civilization of the Renaissance in Italy*. Harmondsworth: Penguin Books.

Campbell, Ian, and John Burgess. 2001. "Casual Employment in Australia and Temporary Employment in Europe: Developing a Cross-National Comparison." *Work, Employment and Society* 15, no. 1: 171–84.

Carmichael, Gordon A. 2002. "Taking Stock at the Millennium: Family Formation in Australia." *Journal of Population Research* 19, no. 1: 91–104.

Castells, Manuel. 1997. *The Power of Identity*. Vol. 2. Malden: Blackwell.

CNIJ (Centro Nacional de Informacao Juvenil). 1997. "International Juvenile Justice and Related Issues." <http://zimmer.csufresno.edu/~haralds/ FOREIGNJUVJUS.htm > (12 December 2005).

Cohen, Phil. 1997. *Rethinking the Youth Question: Education, Labour and Cultural Studies*. London: Macmillan.

Colarusso, Calvin A., and Robert A. Nemiroff. 1981. *Adult Development: A New Dimension in Psychodynamic Theory and Practice*. New York and London: Plenum Press.

Commons, Michael L., Jan D. Sinnott, Francis A. Richards, and Cheryl Armon. 1989. *Adult Development*. New York.

Côté, James E. 2000. *Arrested Adulthood: The Changing Nature of Maturity and Identity*. New York: New York University Press.

Crawford, Kate. (2006). *Adult Themes: Rewriting the Rules of Adulthood*. Sydney: Pan Macmillan.

Creedon, Jeremiah. 1995. "Vanishing Cream for the Mind." <http://www.newint.org/issue264/vanishing.htm> (5 November 2002)

Crouch, Mira, and Heather McKenzie. 2006. "The Logic of Small Samples in Qualitative Research." *Social Science Information* 45: 483–99.

Daily Telegraph. 2002. "And that's Why the Baby is a Vamp." August 22.

Danesi, Marcel. 2003. *Forever Young: The Teen-Aging of Modern Culture*. Toronto: University of Toronto Press.

Davies, Norman. 1996. *Europe: A History*. London: Oxford University Press.

De Vaus, David. 2005. "Australian Families." In *Handbook of World Families*, ed. B. N. Adams, and J. Trost. Thousand Oaks: Sage.

DHA (Department of Health and Ageing). 2003. "Human Ethics Legal Handbook." <http://health. gov.au/nhmrc/hrecbook/03_law/01.htm> (22 April 2004).

Douglas, Mary. 1986. *How Institutions Think*. New York: Syracuse University Press.

Du Bois-Reymond, Manuela. 1998. "I Don't Want to Commit Myself Yet: Young People's Life Concept." *Journal of Youth Studies* 1: 63–79.

Duerr, Hans Peter. 1985. *Dreamline: Concerning the Boundary between Wilderness and Civilization*, trans. F. Goodwin. Oxford: Blackwell.

Durkheim, Emile. 1960. *The Division Of Labor In Society*. New York: Free Press.

———. 1966. *The Rules of Sociological Method*, ed. G.E.G. Catlin, trans. S.A. Solovay and J.H. Mueller. New York: Free Press.

———. 1979. *Suicide: A Study In Sociology*, trans. J. A. Spaulding and G. Simpson, ed. G. Simpson. New York: Free Press.

Duveen, Gerard. 2000. "Introduction: The Power of Ideas." In Serge Moscovici. *Social Representations: Explorations in Social Psychology*, ed. G. Duveen. Cambridge: Polity.

Dwyer, Peter, and Johanna Wyn. 2001. *Youth, Education and Risk: Facing the Future*. London: Routledge.

EGRIS (European Group for Integrated Social Research). 2001. "Misleading Trajectories: Transition Dilemmas of Young Adults in Europe." *Journal of Youth Studies* 4, no. 1: 101–18.

Ehrenberg, Alain. 2004. *Das erschöpfte Selbst: Depression und Gesellschaft in der Gegenwart*. Frankfurt: Campus.

Ehrenreich, Barbara. 2005. *Bait and Switch: The (Futile) Pursuit of the American Dream*. New York: Metropolitan Books.

Eisenstadt, Shmuel. 1971. *From Generation to Generation: Age Groups and Social Structure*. New York: Free Press.

Elder, Glen H. 1985. "Perspectives on the Life Course." In *Life Course Dynamics*, ed. G. Elder. New York: Cornell University Press.

———. 1994. "Time, Human Agency and Social Change: Perspectives on the Life Course." *Sociological Psychology Quarterly* 57: 4–15.

Elias, Norbert. 1978. *The Civilizing Process: The History of Manners*. Vol. 1. Oxford: Blackwell.
——. 1999. *Die Gesellschaft der Individuen*. Frankfurt: Suhrkamp.
Erikson, Erik H. 1950. *Childhood and Society*. New York: Norton.
——. 1968. *Identity: Youth and Crisis*. New York: Norton.
Etzioni, Amatai. 1993. *The Spirit of Community: Rights, Responsibilities and the Communitarian Agenda*. New York: Crown.
Ford, Carol, Abigail English, and Garry Sigman. 2004. "Confidential Health Care for Adolescents: Position Paper of the Society for Adolescent Medicine." *Journal of Adolescent Health* 35, no. 2: 160–67.
Fornäs, Johan, and Goran Bolin. ed. 1995. *Youth Culture in Late Modernity*. London: Sage.
Foucault, Michel. 1994. "Ethics: Subjectivity and Truth." In *The Essential Works of Michel Foucault 1954–1984*, vol. 1, ed. P. Rabinow, trans R. Hurley. New York: New York Press.
Frank, Thomas. 1997. *The Conquest of Cool: Business Culture, Counterculture, And the Rise of Hip Consumerism*. Chicago: University of Chicago Press.
Fraser, Nancy. 1995. "From Redistribution to Recognition? Dilemmas of Justice in a 'Post-Socialist' Age." *New Left Review* 1, no. 212: 68–93.
——. 2000. "Rethinking Recognition." *New Left Review* (May–June): 107–20.
——. 2001. "Recognition without Ethics?" *Theory, Culture & Society* 18, no. 2–3: 21–42.
Freud, Sigmund. 2004 [1930]. *Das Unbehagen in der Kultur und andere kulturtheoretische Schriften*. Frankfurt: Fischer.
Friedenberg, Edgar Z. 1964. *The Vanishing Adolescent*. New York: Dell.
Fromm, Erich. 2001. *The Fear of Freedom*. London: Routledge.
Fukuyama, Francis. 1992. *The End Of History and the Last Man*. London: Hamilton.
Furedi, Frank. 2003. "Children Who Won't Grow Up." <http://www.spiked-online.com/Printable/00000006DE8D.htm> (12 December 2005).
——. 2004. *Therapy Culture: Cultivating Vulnerability in an Uncertain Age*. New York: Routledge.
Furlong, Andy, and Fred Cartmel. 1997. *Young People and Social Change: Individualization and Risk in Late Modernity*. Philadelphia: Open University Press.
Furstenberg, Frank F. 2000. "The Sociology of Adolescence and Youth in the 1990s: A Critical Commentary." *Journal of Marriage and the Family* 62: 896–910.
Furstenberg, Frank F., Sheela Kennedy, Vonnie C. McCloyd, Rubén G. Rumbaut, and Richard A. Settersten. 2003. "Between Adolescence and Adulthood: Expectations about the Timing of Adulthood." The Network of Transitions to Adulthood. Philadelphia: The MacArthur Foundation.
——. 2004. "Growing Up is Harder to Do." *Contexts* 3, no. 3: 33–41.
Galeano, Eduardo. 2000. *Upside Down: Primer for the Looking-Glass World*. New York: Picador.
Garhammer, Manfred. 1999. *Wie Europäer Ihre Zeit Nutzen: Zeitstrukturen und Zeitkulturen im Zeichen der Globalisierung*. Berlin: Edition Sigma.
Giddens, Anthony. 1984. *The Constitution of Society: Outline of The Theory of Structuration*. Berkeley: University of California Press.
——. 1991. *Modernity and Self-Identity: Self and Society in the Late Modern Age*. Oxford and Cambridge: Polity.
——. 1992. *The Transformation of Intimacy: Sexuality, Love and Eroticism in Modern Societies*. Oxford and Cambridge: Polity.
——. 1996. *In Defence of Sociology: Essays, Interpretations and Rejoinders*. Cambridge: Polity.
Gilding, Michael. 2000. *Australian Families: A Comparative Perspective*. Sydney: Longman.
Gillis, John R. 1981. *Youth and History: Traditions and Change in European Age Relations, 1770–Present*. New York: Academic Press.
Giroux, Henry A. 2000. *Stealing Innocence: Corporate Culture's War on Children*. New York: Palgrave.
Goffman, Erving. 1959. *The Presentation of Self in Everyday Life*. New York: Doubleday.
——. 1986. *Stigma: Notes on the Management of Spoiled Identity*. New York: Simon and Schuster.

Gould, Roger L. 1978. *Transformations: Growth and Change in Adult Life*. New York: Simon and Schuster.

Gouliquer, Lynne. 2000. "Pandora's Box: The Paradox of Flexibility in Today's Workplace." *Current Sociology* 48, no. 1: 29–38.

Graubard, Stephen R. 1976. "Preface to the Issue 'Adulthood'" *Daedalus* 105, no. 2: v–viii.

Gross, Neil. 2005. "The Detraditionalization of Intimacy Reconsidered." *Sociological Theory* 23, no. 3 (September): 286–311.

Grumley, John. 1988. "Weber's Fragmentation of Totality." *Thesis Eleven* 21, no. 1: 20–39.

Habermas, Jürgen. 1992. "Individuation through Socialization: On George Herbert Mead's Theory of Subjectivity." In *Postmetaphysical Thinking: Philosophical Essays*. Cambridge: Polity.

Halbwachs, Maurice. 1992. *On Collective Memory*, ed. L. Coser. Chicago: Chicago University Press.

Hall, Stanley G. 1904. *Adolescence: Its Psychology and its Relations to Anthropology, Sociology, Sex, Crime, Religion and Education*. New York: Appleton.

Hall, Stuart, and Tony Jefferson. ed. 1976. *Resistance through Rituals*. London: Hutchinson.

Hamilton, Clive, and Elizabeth Mail. 2003. "Downshifting in Australia: A Sea-Change in the Pursuit of Happiness." *Report* 50. Canberra: Australia Institute.

Hanawalt, Barbara. 1992. "Historical descriptions and Prescriptions for Adolescence," *Journal of Family History* 17, no. 4: 341–51.

Hareven, Tamara. 1978. "The Last Stage: Historical Adulthood and Old Age." In *Adulthood*, ed. E.H. Erikson. New York: Norton.

Harvey, David. 1989. *The Condition Of Postmodernity*. Oxford: Blackwell.

Hegel, Georg W.F. 1983 [1819/1820]. *Grundlinien der Philosophie des Rechts: Die Vorlesung von 1819/20 in einer Nachschrift*, ed. D. Henrich. Frankfurt: Suhrkamp.

Heinz, Walter R., and Helga Krüger. 2001. "Life Course: Innovations and Challenges for Social Research." *Current Sociology* 49, no. 2: 29–54.

Heller, Agnes. 1985. *The Power Of Shame*. London: Routledge.

———. 1993. *A Philosophy of History in Fragments*. Oxford: Blackwell.

———. 1999. *A Theory of Modernity*. Oxford: Blackwell.

Heller, Agnes, and Ferenc Feher. 1988. *The Postmodern Political Condition*. Oxford and Cambridge: Polity.

Herald Sun. 2003. "Kids Who Refuse to Grow Up." December 4.

———. 2004. "'Adults'" Fail the Age Test." August 3.

Hess, Beth. 1988. "Social Structures and Human Lives." In *Social Change and the Life Course*, ed. M.W. Riley, B.J. Huber, and B. Hess. London: Sage.

Hess, Jennifer. 2001. "Preparing to Measure Welfare Reform Using the Longitudinal Survey of Program Dynamics." SPD Analytic Reports. US Department of Commerce, Economics and Statistics Administration. US Census Bureau.

Heywood, Colin. 2001. *A History of Childhood: Children and Childhood in the West from Medieval to Modern Times*. Cambridge: Polity.

Hine, Thomas. 1999. *The Rise and Fall of the American Teenager*. New York: Avon.

Hobsbawm, Erich. 1995. *The Age of Extremes: The Short Twentieth Century 1914–1991*. London: Abacus.

Hockey, Jenny, and Allison James. 1993. *Growing Up and Growing Old: Ageing and Dependency in the Life Course*. London: Sage.

Holtgrewe, Ursula, Stephan Voswinkel, and Gabriele Wagner. 2000. *Anerkennung und Arbeit*. Konstanz: UVK.

Honneth, Axel. 1995a. "Pluralization and Recognition: On the Self-Misunderstanding of Postmodern Social Theories." In *The Fragmented World of the Social: Essays in Social and Political Philosophy*, ed. C.W. Wright. New York: State University of New York Press.

———. 1995b. "Integrity and Disrespect: Principles of a Conception of Morality Based on a Theory of Recognition." In *The Fragmented World of the Social: Essays in Social and Political Philosophy*, ed. C.W. Wright. New York: State University of New York Press.

———. 1996. *The Struggle for Recognition: The Moral Grammar of Social Conflicts*. Cambridge: MIT Press.

———. 2002a. *Befreiung aus der Mündigkeit: Paradoxien des gegenwärtigen Kapitalismus*. Frankfurt: Campus.

———. 2002b. "Organisierte Selbstverwirklichung: Paradoxien der Individualisierung." In *Befreiung aus der Mündigkeit: Paradoxien des gegenwärtigen Kapitalismus*, ed. A. Honneth. Frankfurt: Campus.

———. 2003. "Redistribution as Recognition: A Response to Nancy Fraser." In *Redistribution or Recognition?* trans. J. Golb, J. Ingram, and C. Wilke. London: Verso.

Houellebecq, Michel. 2001. *Atomised*. London: Verso.

Huntington, Samuel. 1996. *The Clash Of Civilizations and the Remaking of World Order*. New York: Simon and Schuster.

Inglehart, Ronald. 1977. *The Silent Revolution: Changing Values and Political Styles among Western Publics*. Princeton: Princeton University Press.

———. 1990. *Culture Shift in Advanced Industrial Societies*. Princeton: Princeton University Press.

Inglehart, Ronald, and Pippa Norris. 2003. *Rising Tide: Gender Equality and Cultural Change Around the World*. Cambridge: Cambridge University Press.

Jacoby, Mario. 1990. *Individuation and Narcissism: The Psychology of the Self in Jung and Kohut*, trans. M. Gubitz and F. O'Kane. London and New York: Routledge.

Jacques, Elliot. 1965. "Death and the Mid-life Crisis." *International Journal of Psycho-Analysis* 46, no. 4: 502–14.

James, Allison and Alan Prout. ed. 1997. *Constructing and Reconstructing Childhood: Contemporary Issues in the Sociological Study of Childhood*. London: Falmer.

Johnson, Leslie. 1989. "The Teenage Girl: The Social Definition of Growing Up for Young Australian Women, 1950 to 1965." *History of Education Review* 18, no. 1: 1–12.

Jordan, Winthrop D. 1978. "Adulthood in America." In *Adulthood*, ed. E. H. Erikson. New York: Norton.

Jung, Carl G. 1977a. *The Collected Works of C. G. Jung*. Vol. 7, trans. R.F.C. Hull. London: Routledge.

———. 1977b. *The Collected Works of C. G. Jung*. Vol. 18, trans. R.F.C. Hull. London: Routledge.

Kant, Immanuel. 1975 [1784]. *Was ist Aufklärung? Aufsätze zur Geschichte und Philosophie*. Göttingen: Vandenhoeck und Ruprecht.

Keniston, Kenneth. 1970. "Youth: A 'New' Stage of Life." *American Scholar* 39, no. 40: 631–54.

Kilmartin, Christine. 2000. "Young Adult Moves: Leaving Home, Returning Home, Relationships." *Family Matters* 55: 34–41.

Kimmel, Douglas C. 1974. *Adulthood and Aging: An Interdisciplinary Developmental View*. New York: Wiley.

Klages, Helmut. 1993. *Traditionsbruch als Herausforderung: Perspektiven der Wertewandelsgesellschaft*. Frankfurt: Campus.

Kohli, Martin. 1986. "The World We Forgot: A Historical Review of the Life Course." In *Later Life: The Social Psychology of Aging*, ed. V.W. Marshall. Beverly Hills: Sage.

———. 1990. "Lebenslauf und Lebensalter als gesellschaftliche Konstruktionen: Elemente zu einem interkulturellen Vergleich." In *Im Lauf der Zeit: Ethnographische Studien zur gesellschaftlichen Konstruktion von Lebensaltern*, ed. G. Elwert. Saarbrücken.

Krüger, Heinz-Hermann, and Hans-Jürgen von Wensierski. 1991. "Jugend-Zeit: Kontinuitäten und Diskontinuitäten in jugendlichen Biographieverläufen." In *Jugend zwischen Moderne und Postmoderne*, ed. W. Helsper. Opladen: Leske und Budrich.

Krüger, Helga, and Bernd Baldus. 1999. "Work, Gender and the Life Course: Social Construction and Individual Experience." *Canadian Journal of Sociology* 24, no. 3: 355–79.

LA Times. 2002. "Hope I Play as I get Old." <http://www.latimes.com/entertainment/printedition/suncalendar/1a-000013979feb24.story> (5 November 2002).

Lacan, Jacques. 1968. "The Mirror-Phase as Formative of the Function of the I." *New Left Review* 51 (September/October): 71–77.

Lane, Robert E. 1991. *The Market Experience*. Cambridge: Cambridge University Press.

Lasch, Christopher. 1979. *The Culture of Narcissism: American Life in an Age of Diminishing Expectations*. New York: Warner.

———. 1984. *The Minimal Self: Psychic Survival in Troubled Times*. New York and London: Norton.

Lee, Nick. 2001. *Childhood and Society: Growing Up in an Age of Uncertainty*. Buckingham: Open University Press.

Lemke, Thomas. 2001. "'The Birth of Bio-Politics'": Michel Foucault's Lecture at the Collège de France on Neo-Liberal Governmentality." *Economy and Society* 30, no. 2: 190–207.

Lenzen, Dieter. 1991. "Moderne Jugendforschung und postmoderne Jugend: Was leistet noch das Identitätskonzept?" In *Jugend zwischen Moderne und Postmoderne*, ed. W. Helsper. Opladen: Leske und Budrich.

Levi, Giovanni, and Jean-Claude Schmitt. 1997. *A History of Young People*. 2 vol. Cambridge and London: Harvard University Press.

Luhmann, Niklas. 1986. *Love as Passion: The Codification of Intimacy*, trans. J. Gaines and D.L. Jones. Cambridge: Polity.

———. 2001. "Notes on Poetry and Social Theory." In *Theory, Culture and Society* 18, no. 1: 15–27.

Lukes, Steven. 1992. *Emile Durkheim: His Life and Work*. Harmondsworth: Penguin.

Macdonald, Fiona, and Sonya Holm. 2002. "Precarious Work, Uncertain Futures: The Experience of 25 to 34-Year-Olds." *Growth*, no. 49: 16–24.

Mackay, Hugh. 1997. *Generations: Baby Boomers, Their Parents and Their Children*. Sydney: Macmillan.

Maguire, Meg, Stephen J. Ball, and Sheila Macrae. 2001. "Post-Adolescence, Dependence and the Refusal of Adulthood." *Discourse* 22, no. 2: 197–211.

Margalit, Avishai. 1996. *The Decent Society*, trans. N. Goldblum. Cambridge: Harvard University Press.

Markus, Gyorgy. 1997. "Antinomies of 'Culture.'" *Essay*. Collegium Budapest. Institute for Advanced Study.

Marwick, Arthur. 1999. *The Sixties: Cultural Revolution in Britain, France, Italy and the United States, c. 1958–c. 1974*. Oxford: Oxford University Press.

May, Michael, and Andreas von Prondczynsky 1991. "Jugendliche Subjektivität im Zeichen der Auflösung des traditionell Politischen." In *Jugend zwischen Moderne und Postmoderne*, ed. W. Helsper. Opladen: Leske und Budrich.

Mayer, Karl-Ulrich, and Walter Müller. 1986. "The State and the Structure of the Life Course." In *Human Development and the Life Course: Multidisciplinary Perspectives*, ed. A.B. Sorensen, F.E. Weinert, and L.R. Sherrod. Hillsdale: Erlbaum.

McDonald, Kevin. 1999. *Struggles for Subjectivity: Identity, Action and Youth Experience*. Cambridge: Cambridge University Press.

McDonald, Peter. 1996. "Young People in Australia Today: A socio-demographic Perspective." In *Mortgaging our Future? Families and Young People in Australia*. Sydney: University of New South Wales.

Mead, George H. 1934. *Mind, Self, and Society*. Chicago: University of Chicago Press.

Mead, Margaret. 1928. *Coming of Age in Samoa: A Psychological Study of Primitive Youth for Western Civilization*. New York: Morrow Quill Paperbacks.

Mead, Rebecca. 2001. "It's All Good." <http://www.reveccamead.com/2001/2001_06_11_comm_nba.htm> (25 November 2003).

Merser, Cheryl. 1987. *Grown-Ups: A Generation in Search of Adulthood*. New York: G.P. Putnam's.

Mirowsky, John, and Catherine E. Ross. 2003. *Social Causes of Psychological Distress*. New York: de Gruyter.

Mitterauer, Michael. 1992. *A History of Youth*, trans. G. Dunphy. Oxford and Cambridge: Blackwell.

Mongardini, Carlo. 1996. "The Culture of the Present." Geschichte und Gegenwart 2: 86–91.

Morris, Colin. 1995. The Discovery of the Individual, 1050–1200. Toronto: Toronto University Press.

Moscovici, Serge. 2000. Social Representations: Explorations in Social Psychology. Cambridge: Polity.

Musgrove, Frank. 1964. Youth and the Social Order. London: Routledge and Kegan Paul.

MX Australia. 2004. "Forever Young Adultescents Won't Grow Up." February 4.

Neugarten, Bernice L. ed. 1964. Personality in Middle and Late Life: Empirical Studies. New York.

Nora, Pierre. 1992. Realms of Memory: Rethinking The French Past, trans. A. Goldhammer, ed. L.D. Kritzman. New York: Columbia University Press.

OED (Oxford English Dictionary). 1989. Oxford: Clarendon.

Offe, Klaus. 1984. Arbeitsgesellschaft: Strukturprobleme und Zukunftsperspektiven. Frankfurt: Campus.

Parsons, Talcott. 1942a. "The Kinship System of the Contemporary United States." In Essays in Sociological Theory. New York: Free Press.

———. 1942b. "Age and Sex in the Social Structure of the United States." In Essays in Sociological Theory. New York: Free Press.

———. 1951. The Social System. London: Routledge and Kegan Paul.

Passerini, Luisa. 1997. "Youth as Metaphor for Social Change: Fascist Italy and America in the 1950s." In A History of Young People: Stormy Evolution to Modern Times, ed. G. Levi and J. Schmitt. Cambridge and London: Harvard University Press.

Peterson, Anders, and Rasmus Willig. 2002. "An Interview with Axel Honneth: The Role of Sociology in the Theory of Recognition." European Journal of Social Theory 5, no. 2: 265–77.

Perec, Georges. 1990. Things: A Story of the Sixties, trans. A. Leak, ed. D. Bellos. Boston: Godine.

Perrot, Michelle. 1997. "Worker Youth: From the Workshop to the Factory." In A History of Young People: Stormy Evolution to Modern Times, ed. G. Levi and J. Schmitt. Cambridge and London: Harvard University Press.

Pike, Bronwyn. 1997. "Work for the Dole: Making Young People Responsible or Blaming the Victims." <http://www.infoxchange.net.au/haasp/workdole.htm> (24 August 2004).

Pilcher, Jane. 1995. Age and Generation in Modern Britain. New York: Oxford University Press.

Pilcher, Jane, John Williams, and Christopher Pole. 2003. "Rethinking Adulthood: Families, Transitions, and Social Change." Sociological Research Online 8, no. 4 <http://www.socresoline.org.uk/8/4/pilcher.html> (24 January 2004).

Postman, Neil. 1982. The Disappearance of Childhood: How TV is Changing Children's Lives. London: Comet.

Pullum, Thomas W., Sara M. Pullum-Piñón, and Myron P. Gutmann. 2002. "Three Eras of Young Adult Home Leaving in Twentieth-Century America." Journal of Social History 35, no. 3: 533–76.

Pusey, Michael. 2003. The Experience of Middle Australia: The Dark Side of Economic Reform. Cambridge: Cambridge University Press.

Qvortrup, Jens. 1994. "Childhood Matters: An Introduction." In Childhood Matters: Social Theory, Practice and Politics, ed. J. Qvortrup, M. Bardy, G. Sgritta, and H. Wintersberger. Aldershot: Avebury.

Riesman, David. 1950. The Lonely Crowd: A Study of the Changing American Character. New Haven: Yale University Press.

Rosa, Hartmut. 1998. "On Defining the Good Life: Liberal Freedom and Capitalist Necessity." Constellations 5: 201–14.

———. 1999. "Bewegung und Beharrung: Überlegungen zu einer sozialen Theorie der Beschleunigung." Leviathan: Zeitschrift für Sozialwissenschaft 27: 386–414.

———. 2003. "Social Acceleration: Ethical and Political Consequences of a Desynchronized High-Speed Society." Constellations 10, no. 1: 3–33.

———. 2001. "Temporalstrukturen in der Spätmoderne: Vom Wunsch nach Beschleunigung und der Sehnsucht nach Langsamkeit. Ein Literaturüberblick in gesellschaftstheoretischer Absicht." Handlung, Kultur, Interpretation 10: 335–381.

Rosenfeld, Anne, and Elizabeth Stark. 1987. "The Prime of Our Lives." Psychology Today 21: 62–72.

Schnapp, Alain. 1997. "Images of Young People in the Greek City-State." In *A History of Young People: Ancient and Medieval Rites of Passage*, ed. G. Levi and J. Schmitt. Cambridge and London: Harvard University Press.

Schroer, Michael. 2000. *Das Individuum der Gesellschaft*. Frankfurt: Suhrkamp.

Schulze, Gerhard. 1992. *Die Erlebnisgesellschaft: Kultursoziologie der Gegenwart*, Frankfurt: Campus.

———. 2003. *Die bester aller Welten: Wohin bewegt sich die Gesellschaft im 21. Jahrhundert?* München: Carl Hanser.

Schütz, Alfred. 1954. "Concept and Theory Formation in the Social Sciences." *Journal of Philosophy* 51, no. 9: 257–73.

———. 1970. *On Phenomenology and Social Relations*, ed. H. Wagner. Chicago: University of Chicago Press.

Schwartz, Seth J., James E. Côté, and Jeffrey J. Arnett. 2005. "Identity and Agency in Emerging Adulthood." *Youth and Society* 37, no. 2: 201–29.

Schwinn, Thomas. 2001. "Staatliche Ordnung und moderne Sozialintegration." *Kölner Zeitschrift für Soziologie und Sozialpsychologie* 53, no. 2: 211–32.

Sennett, Richard. 1992. *The Fall of Public Man*. New York: W.W. Norton.

———. 1998. *The Corrosion of Character: The Personal Consequences of Work in the New Capitalism*. New York and London: Norton.

———. 2006. *The Culture of the New Capitalism*. Yale and London: Yale University Press.

Settersten, Richard A. 2003. "Age Structuring and the Rhythm of the Life Course." In *Handbook Of The Life Course*, ed. J.T. Mortimer and M. Shanahan. New York: Plenum.

Settersten, Richard A., Frank F. Furstenberg, and Rubén G. Rumbaut, ed. 2005. *On the Frontier of Adulthood: Theory, Research, and Public Policy*. Chicago: University of Chicago Press.

Settersten, Richard, and Karl Ulrich Mayer. 1997. "The Measurement of Age, Age Structuring, and the Life Course." *Annual Review of Sociology* 23: 233–61.

Shakespeare, William. 1971. *Complete Works*, ed. W.J. Craig. London: Oxford University Press.

Sheehy, Gail. 1974. *Passages: Predictable Crises of Adult Life*. New York: Dutton.

Smart, Diana, and Ann Sanson. 2003. "Social Competence in Adulthood: Its Nature and Antecedents." *Family Matters* 1, no. 64: 4–9.

Smelser, Neil J. 1980. "Issues of Love and Work in the Study of Adulthood." In *Themes of Love and Work in Adulthood*, ed. N.J. Smelser and E.H. Erikson. Harvard: Harvard University Press.

Soares, Camilo. 2000. "Aspects of Youth, Transitions, and the End of Certainties." *International Social Science Journal* 164: 209–17.

Sørensen, A. 1990. "Unterschiede im Lebensverlauf von Frauen und Männern." *Kölner Zeitschrift für Soziologie und Sozialpsychologie* 31, no. 1: 304–21.

Springhall, John. 1984. "The Origins of Adolescence." *Youth and Policy* 2, no. 3: 20–24.

Statistics Canada. 2001. "2001 Census of Canada." <http://www.12.statcan.ca/English/census01/home/index.cfm> (23 December 2005).

Stevens-Long, Judith. 1988. *Adult Life: Developmental Processes*. Mountain View: Mayfield.

Strausbaugh, John. 2001. *Rock 'til You Drop: The Decline from Rebellion to Nostalgia*. London and New York: Verso.

Sunday Age. 1992. "Adulthood: There is No Law of Consensus." November 29.

Swidler, Ann. 1980. "Love and Adulthood in American Culture." In *Themes of Work and Love in Adulthood*, ed. N.J. Smelser and E.H. Erikson. Harvard: Harvard University Press.

Sydney Morning Herald. 2000. "The Lost Men, Good Weekend Supplement." March 25.

———. 2001a. "Why Today's Teenagers are Growing Up Early." August 20.

———. 2001b. "Life in the Pressure Cooker." August 20.

———. 2005. "60% of Uni Students Live Below Poverty Line." <http://www.smh.com.au/articles/2005/05/14/1116024407236.html> (12 August 2005).

———. 2006. One Family-Sized Job to Go: It's a McRevolution, January 27.

Taylor, Charles. 1991. *The Ethics of Authenticity*. Cambridge: Harvard University Press.

———. 1994. "The Politics of Recognition." In *Multiculturalism: Examining The Politics of Recognition*, ed. A. Gutmann. Princeton: Princeton University Press.

Tiffen, Rodney, and Ross Gittins. 2004. *How Australia Compares*. Melbourne: Cambridge University Press.

Time. 2005a. "Grow Up? Not So Fast." January 25.

———. 2005b. "Parlez-Vous Twixter." January 24.

Todorov, Tzvetan. 1996. *Abenteuer des Zusammenlebens: Versuch einer allgemeinen Anthropologie*. Berlin: Wagenbach.

———. 2003. *Hope And Memory: Reflections on the Twentieth Century*, trans. D. Bellos. London: Atlantic.

Trommler, Frank. 1985. "Mission ohne Ziel: Über den Kult der Jugend im modernen Deutschland." In *Mit uns zieht die Zeit: Der Mythos der Jugend*, ed. T. Koebner, R.-P. Janz, and F. Trommler. Frankfurt: Suhrkamp.

Turner, Jeffrey S., and Donald B. Helms. 1989. *Contemporary Adulthood*. Fort Worth: Rinehart and Winston.

Turner, Victor. 1974. *Dramas, Fields and Metaphors: Symbolic Action in Human Society*. Ithaca: Cornell University Press.

Urbas, Gregor. 2000. "The Age of Criminal Responsibility." In *Trends and Issues in Crime and Criminal Justice*. Canberra: Australian Institute of Criminology.

USCB (United States Census Bureau). 2004a. "Census Bureau Estimates Number of Adults, Older People and School-Age Children in States." <http//:www.census.gov/Press-release/www/releases/archives/population/001703.html> (5 November 2005).

———. 2004b. "Young Adults Living at Home, 1960 to Present." Table AD. <http://www.census.gov/population/socdemo/hh-fam/tabAD-1.pdf> (29 December 2005).

———. 2004c. "Estimated Median Age at First Marriage, by Sex, 1890 to Present." Table MS-2. <http://www.census.gov/population/socdemo/hh-fam/tabMS-2.pdf> (29 December 2005).

Van Gennep, Arnold. 1960. *The Rites of Passage*, trans. M.B. Vizedom and G.L. Caffee. London: Routledge.

von Trotha, Trutz. 1982. "Zur Entstehung von Jugend." *Kölner Zeitschrift für Soziologie und Sozialpsychologie* 34: 254–77.

Voswinkel, Stephan. 2002. "Bewunderung ohne Würdigung?" In *Befreiung aus der Mündigkeit: Paradoxien des gegenwärtigen Kapitalismus*. Frankfurt: Campus.

Wagner, Wolfgang, and Nicky Hayes. 2005. *Everyday Discourse and Common Sense: The Theory of Social Representations*. Basingstoke and New York: Palgrave.

Walker, Martin. 1994. *The Cold War: A History*. New York: Stoddard.

Warde, Alan. 2002. "Consumption, Identity-Formation, and Uncertainty." In *Zygmunt Bauman*, ed. P. Beilharz. London: Sage.

Weber, Max. 1922. *Wirtschaft und Gesellschaft*, ed. Marianne Weber. J.C.B. Mohr (Paul Siebeck): Tübingen.

———. 1992. "Wissenschaft als Beruf." In *Max Weber Gesamtausgabe*, ed. W. J. Mommsen and W. Schluchter. Tübingen: J.C.B. Mohr (Paul Siebeck).

Wilkinson, Helen. 1997. "Kinder der Freiheit: Ensteht eine neue Ethik individueller und sozialer Verantwortung?" In *Kinder der Freiheit*, ed. U. Beck. Frankfurt: Suhrkamp.

Wilkinson, Helen, and Geoff Mulgan. 1995. *Freedom's Children: Work, Relationships, and Politics for 18–34 Year Olds in Britain*. London: Demos.

Williams, Robert R. 1997. *Hegel's Ethics of Recognition*. Berkeley: University of California Press.

Wohlrab-Sahr, Monika. 1992. "Über den Umgang mit biographischer Unsicherheit: Implikationen der 'Modernisierng der Moderne.'" *Soziale Welt* 43, no. 3: 217–36.

Wolff, Kurt H. 1976. *Surrender and Catch: Experience and Inquiry Today*. Dordrecht and Boston.

———. 1983. *Beyond the Sociology of Knowledge: An Introduction and a Development*. New York: Press of America.

———. 1998. *Soziologie der gefährdeten Welt: Zur Rehabilitierung des Individuums*. Frankfurt: Suhrkamp.

Wyn, Johanna. 2004. "Becoming Adult in the 2000s: New transitions and New Careers." *Family Matters* 68 (Winter): 6–12.

Wyn, Johanna, and Rob White. 2000. "Negotiating Social Change: The Paradox of Youth." *Youth and Society* 32, no. 2: 165–83.

Yeats, William B. 1991 [1921]. *Selected Poetry*, ed. T. Webb. London: Penguin.

INDEX

A

adolescence, *See also* delayed adulthood thesis
   conceptual links to historical matura-
      tion, 13
   end of, 21
   homogenization, 69
   preparatory life stage, 11, 73
   prolonged, 19–20, 24, 73, 76
   prominence of, 69
   redefining adulthood, 73
   social scientists' perspectives, 21–22,
      68, 71–72
adolescents
   negative connotations, 65, 70, 74
   as self-conscious social actors, 72–73
Adorno, Theodor, 25, 73, 83–84
adult
   biographical narrative, 83
   as object in sociological investiga-
      tions, 26
   practices and social conditions, 83,
      116
   self-responsibility, 11, 30, 83
   and shifting value system, 83
   and structural insecurities, 44, 48–49,
      83, 118
   usage of term, 11
adult infallibility, 92, 95
adult practices, 13–17
adult recognition, 59
   changing forms, 66–65, 106, 113–14
   institutionalized relations, 61
   market capitalism, 79
   and social change, 59–60, 65
adult roles, 21
adult status
   achievement of, 16, 59–60, 94
   consumption, 78, 93–94
   linked to marriage, 16, 59–60
   objective identifiers, 60

   and self-identification, 52, 60, 61,
      65, 82
adulthood, 101, 103, 118
   association with personhood, 58, 59, 92
   blurring boundaries with adolescence,
      50, 62
   blurring boundaries with childhood,
      35, 50
   commonsense model of, 6
   cultural semantics, 2
   deferring, 19, 20, 24, 112
   emergence as a concept, 10
   entry to, legislation, 18
   growing up without "settling down,"
      101–102
   as heuristic concept, 26
   history, 11–12
   ideological underpinning, 66
   institutionalization of model of, 13
   intersubjective process of social recog-
      nition, 2
   language denoting, 12
   liminality, 74–76, 88
   links to individualization, 11
   marking the beginning, 2
   meanings, 3
      and cultural shifts in meaning
         of love, 43
      denoting stage of life, 11
      history, 11
      individual level changes, 51
      psychologized, 23
      societal level changes, 51
      transformation of youth, 66
   as metaphor for membership in society,
      58–59
   new adulthood, aspects of, 103–104,
      114, 118, 120
   personalization, 61
   postponement, 5, 59, 84

practical redefinition, 10
process of acknowledgment, 2
as psychological state, 4, 61
reconceptualizing, 63–65
redefinition, 7, 63–65, 73, 106, 111,
    114
rejecting, 19, 24, 112
social benchmarks, 2, 112
as social category, 51, 117
as social representation, 10
See also adult recognition; adult status;
    social recognition
"adultness," 11
age
    biological markers, 18, 35
    definitions, 1–2
    delimitations, 1–2, 83
age codification, regulation from, 36
age denoted rights and obligations, 18
age legislation, 18, 36
age norms, 18–19, 36, 83, 107
    consumption, 79–82
    media representation of, 19–20
age of consent, 18
age of criminal responsibility, 18
ageism, 19
anomie, modern, 33–34
"anticipatory socialization," 37
Ariès, Philippe, 56
Arnett, Jeffrey J., 20, 21–22, 23, 24, 49–50,
    59, 75
assimilation, 57
Australia, commonalities with United States,
    6–7
Australian Bureau of Statistics (ABS), 1–2,
    40, 41, 83
authentic life, 28, 31, 33, 42, 78, 95, 101, 114

B
"baby boomer" generation, 15, 39, 70–71, 72,
    73, 81, 115
Bauman, Zygmunt, 7, 8, 25, 26, 28, 29, 31, 32,
    39, 42, 43, 46, 63, 65
Beck, Ulrich, 14, 29, 30, 31, 32, 37, 39, 43, 44,
    46, 47, 62
Beck-Gernsheim, Elisabeth, 29, 30, 32, 47, 62
behavioral sciences, reconceptualization of
    youth, 68
Berger, Peter, 9, 21, 37, 45, 74
Bernstein, Basil, 85
Bildungsroman, 61, 97
biographies
    change in trajectory, 7, 44
    choice, 47–48
    differentiation to life course, 35

fragmentation, 45
impact of life course on, 36–37
as individual's responsibility, 29, 30,
    33, 100
standard, 37–38, 44–45, 57
biological maturity
    as culturally specific, 12
    at younger ages over time, 18, 35
biological sciences, reconceptualization of
    youth, 68
blended families, 40
Bourdieu, Pierre, 69
bourgeois youth, 67

C
Calvinist predestinarianism, 11
capitalism, relations of recognition, 79
careers, 39, 44, 62, 78, 100, 101
childbirth, age of women at, 40
childhood
    blurring boundaries with adulthood,
    35, 50
    as framed by dependency, 58
    standard biography, 38
childless women, 40
children
    as "human becomings," 12
    institutionalization into life course, 47
    preindustrial Europe, 11
choice biography, 47–48
choices. *See* options
cohabitation
    outside of marriage, 42
    young people in parental home, 41
Cold War, impact on youth attitudes, 15
"collective consciousness," 34
collective identity, 28
collective psychology, 52
collective relationship, 52
"collective representations"
    Durkheim's use of term, 9, 10
Coming of Age in Times of Uncertainty
    methodology, 5–6, 84
    respondents
        fatalism, 102–104, 105
        generational identification,
        98–101, 103
        individuation, 95–97
        parenthood, 106–109
        perceptions of adulthood,
        86–87, 88
        perceptions of childhood, 87
        perceptions of independence,
        89–90, 91

perceptions of power, 90
presentation of self, 91–97
sampling, 83, 84, 85
situations, 85–86, 119–20
structure, 7–8
commitment and stability
weighed against independence and
flexibility, 43–44
commitment (intimate relationships), 42
commodity market, 62
commonsense
interaction with social scientific
knowledge, 10
commonsense knowledge
relationship to sociology, 25
commonsense typifications
adult status, attributed, 84
consumer-corporate interests, and "default
individualization," 23
consumption
actualization of personhood, 78–79
adult status, 78
age norms, 79–82
individuals' dissatisfaction and, 77,
79, 82
social recognition, 62, 79, 81
young people, 70, 73
See also options
contemporary young adults. See adults
Côté, James, 3, 20, 22–23, 49, 61, 77
counterculture, 72–73
critical theory, 26, 51, 54, 118
Cuban Missile Crisis (1962), 15
cultural sensibilities, 62
"culture industry," 73, 76, 115

D

"de facto marriages," 42
"de-temporalization of life," 44
"default individualization," 23
delayed adulthood thesis, 20, 21, 24, 50, 59,
65, 112
delinquency, 70
depression, link to individualization, 30
"developmental individualization," 23
developmental psychology, 4, 11, 68
deviance, 19, 70, 113
age norms, 18, 73
"disenchanted" world, 29
disrespect, 56–57
divorce, 40, 42
Durkheim, Emile, 2, 9, 10, 33, 34, 35, 36

E

"early adulthood," 21, 22

education
changing image of youth, 68
entering workforce before end of, 39
government policy, 39
school, 18, 39, 47
separating young from work, 12, 67
standard biography, 39
transition to work, 24
Eisenstadt, Shmuel, 16, 58
Elias, Norbert, 26, 29, 32
"emerging adulthood," 21, 23
employment
forms of, 40
long-term, 15, 39, 45, 61, 62, 77, 100, 101
Enlightenment, 13
epistemological fallacy of late modernity, 23,
103
equality in relationships, 42, 62
Erikson, Erik H, 20, 60, 71, 72, 95
"ethics of authenticity," 85
"ethics of responsibility," 105
existential reassurance of choice, 32–33

F

family household formation, 40–41, 99, See
also blended families; same-sex parents
fatalism, 104–106
new, difference to premodernity,
104–105, 116
fertility levels, 40
Fichte, Johann Gottlieb, 54
flexibility, 82, 114
biographical, 44
intimate relationships, 43, 61–61
labor market, 62, 81
social imperative, 62–63, 65
social relationships, 61
as virtue, 46
flexibilization of work, 40, 44, 47, 62
Fordism, 14, 61
formal age norms, 19, 83
Foucault, Michel, 13, 31
freedom of choice, 32, 33. See also options
Freud, Sigmund, 4
Fromm, Erich, 64
Furstenberg, Frank F., 15, 17, 20, 21, 22, 24, 67
future
foreclosed, 49
individuals, control over, 33, 34
open, 33, 34, 74, 102, 103–104
optimism, 103, 110
planning for, 37, 45–46

G

Giddens, Anthony, 25–26, 42, 43, 46, 105

globalization, social relations, 29
Goffman, Erving, 53, 54, 62, 92, 94, 106
"Golden Age," 13, 15, 46, 61, 79
"governmentality," 31

H

Habermas, Jürgen, 29, 54
Halbwachs, Maurice, 49
Hall, G. Stanley, 11, 13, 72
Hegel, G.W.F., 51, 54–55, 79
Heller, Agnes, 33, 56, 104
heterosexual nuclear family ideal, 14
Hobsbawm, Eric, 13, 46, 73
home ownership, 17, 41
homogenization
        across age groups, 81
        young people, 69
Honneth, Axel, 8, 30, 48, 51, 53, 54
        typology, 55–57, 61
Houellebecq, Michel, 90–91
household formation, 40–41, See also blended
        families; same–sex parents
human development, perspectives, 13
humanity, theory of social recognition, 2

I

I and Me, reconciliation, 55
"ideal of authenticity," 28, 42
ideal types, 24
"identity capital," 23
"identity crisis," 72
identity formation
        adulthood positioned in relation to, 4
        and life course, 36–38
        social-psychological perspective, 55
        social trends determined against, 4
        as struggle between society and
            individual, 52
"immanentization of transcendence," 33
independent living, as marker of adulthood,
        17, 60
"individualism of self-fulfillment," 111
individualization
        contemporary, 29–34
        control over future, subject to indi-
            vidual action, 33, 104
        dependencies, 30
        institutional connections, 30–31
        links to adulthood, 11
        process of, 23
"individualized society," 7
individuals
        control over their life, 33, 34, 104
        destinies and institutional demands,
            30–1

emergence of identity, 28
freedom, 28, 29, 31, 32, 33, 42, 51, 54,
        88, 90, 93, 100, 103, 108, 109, 117
memories, socially derived, 49
orientation towards present, 45
responsibility, 4, 11, 16, 29–30, 31, 63,
        72, 89, 90, 96, 102, 105, 108
        See also biographies; options
individuation. See also personal growth
        contemporary perception, 90, 95, 115,
            118
        and freedom, 29
        Jung's vision, 52–53, 55, 95
infantilisation, contemporary society, 20, 38,
        58
informal age norms, 18, 19, 83
"institutionalized individualism," 29
institutions, and temporal securities, 44, 48, 49
intergenerational relationships, 115–16
intimate relationships, 42–43

J

job insecurity, 39, 40, 41
Jung, Carl Gustav, 52–53, 55, 74, 95
Jungian psychology, 74
juvenile delinquent, social construction, 69–70

K

Kant, Immanuel, 13, 28
"the knowledge society," 39
Kohli, Martin, 35, 36, 37, 44, 48

L

"le mal de l'infini," 33, 34
leaving home. see independent living
life course, 3, 7, 8, 12
        and age, 18
        as defined in social practices, 4
        deinstitutionalization, 44–50
        differentiated from biography, 35
        impact on individuals' biographies,
            36–37
        institutionalized, 36, 37
        post Second World War, 14–15
        segmenting into units, 11
        and social integration, 36
life cycle
        ego-psychology, 72
        Shakespeare's representation of, 34–35
life planning, 46
life stage
        between adolescence and adulthood, 21
        adolescence as preparatory, 11
        adulthood conceptualised as, 11
        consensus, lack of, 83

differentiation, 11–12
personalization, 22
use of term, 4
liminality, 74, 75–76
"linked lives," 37
living arrangements, 41
"loss of innocence," 91, 96, 97
love
    as social recognition, 55–56
    of youth (Western mind), 66, 81
love ideology, 43
Luhmann, Niklas, 5, 33

M

markers of adulthood, 2, 101
    classic, 16–17, 18, 23, 50, 59, 79,
        112–13
    individualization, 49
    post-Second World War, 14–15,
        60–61
    relationship to age, 18–19
    timing, 17–19, 23
    See also independent living; marriage;
        parenthood; work
markers of transition
    individually identified, 49–50, 61
market
    perpetuation of discontent, 77, 79, 82
    for teenagers, 71, 73
market capitalism, 79
marketing
    consumer demographics, 20
    youth culture, 71, 73, 76–77
marriage
    age of first, 40, 41–42
    as marker of adulthood, 16, 59–60, 99
    women, 59–60
maturity
    definition, 21, 74
    law, pluralist conception of, 18
    links to historical process, 13
    notions of, 12–13, 96
Mead, George Herbert, 54, 55
Mead, Margaret, 12, 69
media discourse on adulthood, 5
men
    labor market insecurities, 85
    living with parents, 41
    social recognition, 64
midlife crisis, 4
midlife period, literature, 4
milestones. *See* markers of adulthood
Mill, John Stuart, 123
Moscovici, Serge, 9, 10
music, 76, 80–81

N

nation-state, as identity-conferring entity, 29
"the natural attitude," 26
neoliberalism, 31, 52, 116
new adulthood, definition, 121n3
new adults, definition, 121n3
New Capitalism, 14
"new fatalism," 34
1970s, social transformation, 44
nonsexist attitudes, 62
normal biography, 37
normative lag, standard adulthood and con-
    temporary realities, 10, 24–25, 63, 113

O

OECD countries, 39, 40, 41, 42
old age
    as framed by dependency, 58
    standard biography, 38
options
    perception of, 32, 34, 74–75
    proliferation, 31–32, 33, 34, 49, 74, 76,
        79, 100–101
    surplus, 48
    and transcendence, 32, 34

P

paradox of "accelerated standstill," 45
parenthood
    as lifelong endeavour, 12
    as marker of adulthood, 17, 18, 60,
        106–109
    and social validation, 16
Parsons, Talcott, 19, 20, 29, 69, 71–72
Parsons' (1951) rule, 19
Perec, Georges, 78, 81
personal development, 48, 74, 75, 88, 101,
    111, 115
personal growth, 42, 43, 48, 52, 62, 74, 75, 79,
    82, 111, 116
personhood, 8, 58, 64, 78, 92, 95
    and social inequality, 58, 117
Pilcher, Jane, 3–4, 12, 16, 59
planning, generational shift, 46–47, 99–100,
    102–103, 108–109
pop culture, 23
pop psychology, 52, 111
post-1970 generation
    adult characteristics, 43–44
    expansion of youth, 81–82
"post-adolescence," 20, 68–69
post-Second World War, 10
    delinquency, 70
    markers of adulthood, 14–15, 17,
        59, 113

model of adulthood, 13, 14
standard biography, 38
teenagers, 70–71, 72
transformation, value orientations, 43, 115
transition to adulthood, 20–22
"postmaterialist" attitudes, 43, 75
"practical consciousness," 26
pre-scientific interests, 25, 84
"prescientific thinking," 25
presentism, 46
procreation, as marker of adulthood, 18, 99
productive age, 48
psychological approaches to adulthood, 4
psychological individual, 52
psychological maturity, 11
as culturally specific, 12
psychologists, interest in adult "life stage," 4
psychosocial development
adulthood positioned in relation to, 4
social trends determined against, 4
psychotherapy, 53
puberty, 18

R
"recipe knowledge," 37
recognition. See social recognition
recognition deficit, 59, 63, 64, 82, 113, 115
"reflexivity" (contemporary modernity), 46
remarriage, 42
Renaissance, 28
Riesman, David, 55, 72
rites of passage, 2, 49, 74
absence of, 18
rock stars, 73, 80
Rolland, Romain, 122
Romanticism, 74, 76
Rosa, Hartmut, 32, 44, 45, 78, 79
Rousseau, Jean-Jacques, 61

S
same-sex marriages, 42
same-sex parents, 40
school education, 39
Schütz, Alfred, 25, 26, 37, 106
"second order typifications," 25, 26
Second World War, adulthood in public consciousness, 12
self-centeredness, 110
self-centering, self-centeredness, 110
self-confidence, 15, 53, 56, 88
self-determination, 28, 30, 58, 59
self-esteem, 48, 53, 61
loss, 56–57
theory of social recognition, 2

self-identification, 3, 37, 45, 52, 53, 55, 60, 61, 65, 82, 107
self-perception, 3, 8, 53, 60, 109, 112, 113
self-realization, 30, 42, 43, 52, 54, 79
driving force of individuation, 53
self-recognition, 59, 106
self-respect, 53, 56, 61, 94, 116
self-responsibility, 11, 30, 83
self-understanding, 4, 13, 15, 28, 55, 59, 60, 66, 109, 114
self-worth, theory of social recognition, 2
Sennett, Richard, 14
Shakespeare, William, 11, 34
Simmel, Georg, 54
Smelser, Neil J., 3
social conditions
contemporary life, 77, 82, 83
1960s, 14
social constitution, 3
clarification of, 17–18
communications, 10
social control, early forms, 36
social crises, perceptions of, 30
social fact, 35, 36
social inequality, 62
social integration, 36
critical factors, 37
young people, 69–70
social maturity, 12, 61
social problems, perceived as personal failure, 29–31
social recognition. See also adult recognition;
Honneth, Axel - typology; markers of
adulthood
attained through *parenthood*, 16
changes, traditional to modern societies, 56
concept, in sociology, 53, 54
consumer lifestyles, 62
consumption, 62
and contemporary young adults, 51
and critical theory, 54, 118
gendered, 59–60, 61
Hegel's struggle for, 54, 55
institutionalized, 56
legislative, 56
nonsexist attitudes, 62
quest in marketplace, 62, 76–79, 82
shift in modernity, 54
social practice against residual normative ideals, 63–64
striving for, 55
supply/demand dynamics, 62, 77, 79
at work, 64
social recognition theory, 2, 8, 53–57

"social representations"
  enacting differences, 10
  Moscovici's definition, 9–10
social scientific knowledge, interaction with
  commonsense, 10
social transformations, 39–44
  intergenerational to intragenerational
    mode, 44
  See also education; family household
    formation; living arrangements;
    household formation; marriage;
    work
society
  as entity existing outside individual, 52
  as "institutionalized recognition order," 51
sociological perspective
  contrast to psychological approach, 3
  methodology within the text, 5–6
sociologists, practical consciousness, 26–27
sociology
  adulthood central to, 26, 58, 117–18
  alleged postponement of adulthood,
    4–5, 84
  and common sense knowledge, 25
  derth of studies on adulthood, 3–4, 117
  paradoxical status of adulthood, 26–27
  and "prescientific thinking," 25, 84
"solidarity," 56
standard adulthood, 13, 15–16, 17, 47, 50, 59,
  64, 73, 75
  careers, 62
  devolution, 77
  as normative ideal, 61, 80–81, 101, 107
  normative lag, contemporary realities,
    10, 24–25, 63, 113
  standard biography as model for, 38
  used as benchmark, 23–24
standard biography, 37–38
  education, 39
  work, 38, 39
subjectivization, 23
Swidler, Ann, 43, 111

T
Taylor, Charles, 28, 42, 51, 54, 85, 111
teenagers, 70–71, 77
teleological model of adulthood, evaluation
  young people's practices, 4
"temporalization," 36
transition to adulthood
  and individualistic culture, 22
  social-scientific analysis, 20–22, 25
  timing, 17–19, 24
tripartite biography, 37, 39, 55

Turner, Victor, 74
Twelfth Night (Shakespeare), 11

U
uncertainty
  normalization, 7, 65, 100, 101,
    103–104, 110
  "surrender" notion, 104–105
United Kingdom
  childless women, 40
  living arrangements (young people), 41
  youth subcultures, 70
United States
  adolescence, 20, 21, 22, 70, 72
  age based laws, 18
  childless women, 40
  delinquency, 70
  expansion of youth, 81–82
  history of adulthood, 11, 12, 17, 22,
    76, 81
  living arrangements (young people),
    41, 84
  marriage, 17, 42
university students, 84, 85
U.S. Census Bureau, age definitions, 2, 83
"utopia of natural life," 67

V
value orientations, transformation across
  generations, 43
value research, consensus among social scientists, 43
van Gennep, Arnold, 74, 76

W
Weber, Max, 24, 29, 33, 36, 54, 62
Western societies, self-understanding, 66
Wolff, Kurt, 104–105
women
  childless, 40
  infantilization, 58
  living with parents, 41
  marriage, 17, 40, 42, 59–60, 70–71
  recognition, 61
work
  age at entry, 39
  choices, 48
  deregulation, 39–40
  entering, before end of education, 39
  learning for security at, 39
  as marker of adulthood, 17, 60
  standard biography, 38, 39
  See also employment
workforce flexibility, 40
working-class youth, 67, 70

Wyn, Johanna, 23, 24, 39

Y

young adulthood
    media representation of, 19–20
    social scientists, concepts of, 20, 25
    use of term, 21
young people
    consumerism, 70, 73
    homogenization, 69
    orientation toward peer group, 70,
      71, 72
    redefinition of youth, 68
    subcultural differentiation, 70
youth
    de-differentiation, 80, 81
    definitions, 67
    expansion of, 74–79

    "good time" attitude, 15
    qualities, 74, 75–76, 77, 82
    reconceptualization by sciences,
      68–69
    1950s, 70, 71, 72–73, 76
    1960s-1970s, 15, 39, 70–71, 72, 73,
      81, 115
    stage of life, 67, 74, 76
    transformation in history of, 66, 67–68,
      69, 80
    as transitional category, 67
    See also adolescence; teenagers
youth culture, 70–71, 76
youth labor market, 41
youth subculture, 70, 76. *See also* countercul-
    ture
"youth transitions," 22
youthfulness. *See* youth - qualities